*Routledge Revivals*

# Gender and Qualitative Research

Published in 1996, this book gathers together an original collection of papers on gender and qualitative research. The contributors draw on a variety of research methods and research settings to demonstrate the value of a qualitative approach for studying gender related issues. Individual chapters include discussions on participant observation, ethnographic interviewing, focus groups and the analysis of documentary sources. The volume as a whole reflects the wide range of gender focused work which is ongoing in Cardiff – covering issues such as occupational cultures, violence, genetics and risk, the life cycle and time.

This book was originally published as part of the *Cardiff Papers in Qualitative Research* series edited by Paul Atkinson, Sara Delamont and Amanda Coffey. The series publishes original sociological research that reflects the tradition of qualitative and ethnographic inquiry developed at Cardiff. The series includes monographs reporting on empirical research, edited collections focussing on particular themes, and texts discussing methodological developments and issues.

# Gender and Qualitative Research

Edited by Jane Pilcher and Amanda Coffey

First published in 1996
by Ashgate Publishing Ltd

This edition first published in 2018 by Routledge
2 Park Square, Milton Park, Abingdon, Oxon, OX14 4RN
and by Routledge
711 Third Avenue, New York, NY 10017

*Routledge is an imprint of the Taylor & Francis Group, an informa business*

© 1996 Jane Pilcher and Amanda Coffey

All rights reserved. No part of this book may be reprinted or reproduced or utilised in any form or by any electronic, mechanical, or other means, now known or hereafter invented, including photocopying and recording, or in any information storage or retrieval system, without permission in writing from the publishers.

**Publisher's Note**
The publisher has gone to great lengths to ensure the quality of this reprint but points out that some imperfections in the original copies may be apparent.

**Disclaimer**
The publisher has made every effort to trace copyright holders and welcomes correspondence from those they have been unable to contact.

A Library of Congress record exists under LCCN: 96084602

ISBN 13: 978-1-138-48047-6 (hbk)
ISBN 13: 978-1-351-06278-7 (ebk)
ISBN 13: 978-1-138-48050-6 (pbk)

# Gender and Qualitative Research

*Edited by*
JANE PILCHER
*Department of Sociology, University of Leicester*
AMANDA COFFEY
*School of Social and Administrative Studies*
*University of Wales, Cardiff*

# Avebury

Aldershot • Brookfield USA • Hong Kong • Singapore • Sydney

© J. Pilcher and A. Coffey 1996

All rights reserved. No part of this publication may be reproduced, stored in a retrieval system, or transmitted in any form or by any means, electronic, mechanical, photocopying, recording or otherwise without the prior permission of the publisher.

Published by
Avebury
Ashgate Publishing Limited
Gower House
Croft Road
Aldershot
Hants GU11 3HR
England

Ashgate Publishing Company
Old Post Road
Brookfield
Vermont 05036
USA

**British Library Cataloguing in Publication Data**

Gender and qualitative research. - (Cardiff papers ; 8)
    1. Sex role - Research
    I. Pilcher, Jane II. Coffey, Amanda, 1967-
    305.3'072

    ISBN 1 85972 199 0

**Library of Congress Catalog Card Number:** 96-84602

# Contents

| | |
|---|---|
| *Notes on editors and contributors* | vii |
| *Acknowledgements* | ix |

| | | |
|---|---|---|
| Introduction | | 1 |
| *Jane Pilcher and Amanda Coffey* | | |
| 1. | Masculinity in prison | 6 |
| | *Keith Carter* | |
| 2. | Coping with pit closure in the 1990s: Women's perspectives | 22 |
| | *Bella Dicks* | |
| 3. | From 'honorary chap' to mother: Combining work in the professions with motherhood | 44 |
| | *Janet Stephens* | |
| 4. | Childish things: Men, ageing and violence | 61 |
| | *Julie Owen* | |
| 5. | Chance to choice: Two generations of reproductive decision making | 77 |
| | *Evelyn P. Parsons* | |
| 6. | In the company of other women: A case study of menopause support groups | 98 |
| | *Trish Harding* | |

7.  Focus groups, young people and sex education
    *Lesley Pugsley*                                        114

8.  Men and feminist research
    *Mark Jones*                                            131

9.  Time for feminist approaches to technology, 'nature' and
    work
    *Barbara Adam*                                          149

# Notes on editors and contributors

**Barbara Adam** teaches social theory and women's studies at the University of Wales, Cardiff. She has published extensively on the social study of time including *Time and Social Theory* (1990) (Polity) which was awarded the Philip Abrams memorial prize and *Time Watch* (1995) (Polity) which was awarded the J T Fraser prize. For the period 1994-96 she holds an ESRC fellowship to research the complex temporalities of environmental processes and their social impact. She is founder editor of *Time and Society*.

**Keith Carter** completed his doctorate at the University of Wales, Cardiff. His research was on the occupational culture of prison officers and included an ethnography of a provincial prison setting.

**Amanda Coffey** is a lecturer in the Sociology at the University of Wales, Cardiff. She has published in the areas of gender, occupational socialisation and research methods. She is co-author (with Paul Atkinson) of *Making Sense of Qualitative Data* (1996 Sage). She is currently working on a new project on gender, sexuality and fieldwork.

**Bella Dicks** is a tutorial fellow at the School of Social and Administrative Studies, University of Wales, Cardiff where she is carrying out doctoral research into heritage representations of mining communities. She was previously employed as a research assistant at Sheffield Hallam University on the ESRC *Management of Personal Welfare Initiative* project 'Coping with Pit Closure in Britain's Ex-Mining Communities', co-directed by Chas Critcher and David Waddington.

**Trish Harding** completed a higher degree in the School of Social and Administrative Studies, University of Wales, Cardiff. She currently works at the University of the West of England at Bristol.

**Mark Jones** is the Community Health Adviser at the Royal College of Nursing. He is responsible for policy formation and practice development in respect of community nursing practice. He is particularly interested in the relationship between general practice and nursing, with an emphasis on gender and the power dynamics between these groups, and the move for nursing to become more autonomous and self-accountable. He has written a number of journal papers on these themes.

**Julie Owen** was a PhD student in the School of Social and Administrative Studies, University of Wales, Cardiff. Her research focused on gender and violence. She is currently teaching in Hampshire.

**Evelyn P. Parsons** is a lecturer and a research fellow at the University of Wales College of Medicine in Cardiff, with an interest in psychosocial genetics. She is currently responsible for the evaluation of the All Wales Newborn screening programme for Duchenne Muscular dystrophy. As a medical sociologist she has a specific interest in the social construction of genetic risk and the psychosocial implications of presymptomatic genetic testing, specifically in the field of familial breast cancer.

**Jane Pilcher** is a lecturer in sociology at the University of Leicester. She undertook her doctoral research at Cardiff. She has published in the areas of young people, gender and generations. Her recent publications include *Age and Generation in Modern Britain* (1995: Oxford University Press).

**Lesley Pugsley** is a higher degree student at the University of Wales, Cardiff, funded by the ESRC. Her project is on higher education and markets. Her other research interests include educational policy and sex education.

**Janet Stephens** is a lecturer in Family Studies at the University of Wales, Cardiff. She also teaches on gender relations and women's studies courses. Her higher degree research focuses on women doctors' experiences as mothers who work in the professions.

# Acknowledgements

The production of this book has been supported by a number of individuals and organisations. The research which is reported on has received financial help from the Economic and Social Research Council and the University of Wales (Studentships). The chapters draw on fieldwork in a range of settings. We would like to acknowledge all the research sites and individuals which granted access to the contributors of this volume.

The editors would like to thank ARENA Publishing (Australia) for permission to reprint Barbara Adam's chapter, *Time for Feminist approaches to technology, 'nature' and work.* This first appeared in *ARENA*, volume 4 (1994/95).

Jackie Swift turned the chapters into camera-ready copy with considerable skill and we are very grateful to her. We would also like to thank Joanna Wilkes who undertook a lot of the editorial administration. Paul Atkinson helped with the final editorial work on some chapters. Lesley Pugsley helped to finalise biographical details on individual chapters. Eddie May and Julian Pitt have provided advice and support throughout the project.

The interpretations and opinions reported on in the chapters are those individual authors and do not necessarily represent those of the various agencies acknowledged above.

# Introduction

*Jane Pilcher and Amanda Coffey*

This book contains a collection of papers written by individuals who are or have been associated with the University at Cardiff; as postgraduates, staff members and research collaborators. The papers, as a collection, give an overview of the wide variety of ethnographic and qualitative research which has been undertaken on gender. While the collection does not exhaust the diversity of 'gender' work which has been connected with Cardiff, it does give an indication of the theoretical, methodological and empirical underpinnings and interests which have guided much of the research. The book reflects both the qualitative tradition at Cardiff, and the vitality of current work in the broad area of gender.

The volume as a whole draws on two trends in British sociology. The first of these is the amount of research endeavour now dedicated to the sociological analyses of gender. While our sociological data base and knowledge is still far from complete, we now have a much better understanding of gender relations and the sexual politics of everyday life. Research on women, influenced by a strong feminist theoretical framework, has more recently been joined by a small, but rapidly expanding, corpus of research and theoretical development in the areas of men's studies, masculinities, queer theory and sexualities. Work at Cardiff has drawn on these developments; providing insights into masculinity, femininity and sexuality, and utilising a range of feminist and gender theories.

Alongside the empirical interest in gender there has ensued a persuasive debate about the appropriate social research methods for the study of women, and gender more generally. Feminist epistemologies and feminist methods have been central to this debate. While it is too simplistic (and indeed wrong) to suggest that feminist methods or 'gender sensitive' methods are naturally and obviously qualitative, many researchers (feminist and otherwise) have pointed to the appropriateness of qualitative methods for the study of gender and sexuality. While the jury is perhaps still out on what does and what does not constitute feminist methods *per se*, research on gender (and women more particularly) has prompted a reconceptualization of what constitutes appropriate and sensitive research methods. The contributors to this book use a wide variety of qualitative methods to explore a range of topics concerned with gender relations and gendered experiences. While some explicitly refer to feminist methods (equally some do not), all of them demonstrate and discuss the appropriateness of their chosen methods for researching gender.

In this introduction we do not plan to recapitulate each chapter in great detail. Rather, we attempt to draw attention to the main analytic and methodological themes which appear throughout the book. These are not in any particular order of emphasis or importance.

While adopting a broadly qualitative perspective to their research endeavours, the contributors to the book demonstrate the use of a wide variety of social research methods. Indeed it is testimony to the growth of interest in qualitative research methods that the variety is now so great. The different research methods are all discussed by the authors in the specific context of gender and research. Individual chapters include discussions on participant observation, interviewing and the collection of written texts. For example, Carter's ethnography of the male prison setting included observation and ethnographic interviews. His chapter demonstrates how observing and taking part in informal conversations can capture both the 'personal' and the public faces of a social setting. He discusses how his research enabled him to consider how masculinities are reproduced, maintained and displayed with the institutional environment.

Indepth, ethnographic interviews were undertaken by a number of our contributors. In different contexts they reveal that 'letting people talk' is a powerful way of understanding relationships between genders and generations. Dicks conducted a series of interviews in (ex)mining communities. In her chapter for this book she uses data collected from interviews with women in these communities to explore the inter-connectedness of the private world of the home and the public world of work. In particular she considers the consequences of community unemployment for private, gendered relationships. Stephens interviewed women who were combining professional careers with motherhood. Like Dicks, she explores key life transitions and how social actors (in this case women) make sense of those transitions; developing strategies to account for and cope with them. The chapter by Parsons also explores motherhood, this time in the context of reproductive decision making. She interviewed mothers and daughters of families with a genetic risk, and explored their accounting devices and decision strategies. Owen's chapter reports research on masculinity and violence. She interviewed both men and women. In the chapter in this volume she considers how male violence is talked about, accounted for and mediated by age. While the chapters by Dicks, Stephens, Owen and Parsons span a range of empirical topics (unemployment and domestic life; professional and motherhood roles; masculinity and violence; genetics and reproduction), they collectively demonstrate the potential of qualitative interviewing and 'talking' for the collection of gendered stories on potentially sensitive topic areas.

Focus group interviews were conducted by Pugsley and by Jones. Both were able to assess the benefits and problems of collecting data via collective group discussions. Both authors give very vivid descriptions of focus group interviews with social actors they did not readily identify with. As a mature research student Pugsley conducted interviews with sixth form students about sex education. Jones (a man) interviewed female practice nurses about their training needs. Pugsley and Jones found focus group interviews provided a useful way of 'giving voice' to their research subjects. Harding asked her informants to write narratives for her and worked with this textual data to analyse how women account for their coping strategies. Her research focused on menopausal support groups in England and Scotland. Her collection of textual data 'by post' demonstrates that it is possible to work with qualitative and feminist research ideals without face-to-face interactions. This serves to broaden our conceptions of appropriate methods for researching gender.

The different chapters (and the research projects to which they refer) all demonstrate the centrality of the personal in research. The range of research methods enabled narratives and accounts to be collected, many in social actors' own voices, language and words. How individuals make sense of their lives and experiences was a primary research focus. The contributors present multiple voices and perspectives; highlighting multiple realities of complex social worlds. For example Parsons presents the voices of mothers *and* daughters (almost a dialogue), as they retrospectively and prospectively assess their genetic reproductive risks. Owen uses both male *and* female voices, and different generational voices to explore the phenomenon of male violence. Dicks 'gives voice' to women who are experiencing the consequences of male mass unemployment. Pugsley's chapter on young people's views on sex education contrasts formal and informal realities of sex education in schools, and demonstrates that male and female students construct different accounts of their experiences. What is also clear from some of the contributors' accounts is that the researcher is omnipresent in the research process. Jones' paper, for example, is a highly reflective account of a man researching women from a sympathetic, and in his words, feminist perspective.

Several of the chapters are concerned with demonstrating the 'gender work' that goes on in social actors' everyday lives and experiences. How gender 'gets done' and how it is understood by individual social actors is a key aspect of the chapters by Owen, Carter and Dicks in particular. Owen shows how violence is accounted for in the context of the reproduction of masculine identities. She demonstrates that men and women do a substantial amount of gender work in the construction of their social and gendered identities. Carter's chapter explores how male prisoners and male prison officers both conform to particular forms of masculinity. He discusses the ways in which masculinity is reproduced and maintained through prison interactions. The chapter by Dicks shows how women deconstruct and reconstruct their identities - as women, wives, mothers and workers, within the post-mining community. These chapters all give insight into the practical *and* the narrative gender work which individual social actors engage in, in order to demonstrate, maintain, reproduce, justify themselves and others as male and female, masculine and feminine.

A further theme contained within the collection is the relationship between gender and the life course. The chapters by Harding, Parsons and Stephens, especially, deal with women and life-course transitions. Harding's chapter on menopausal support groups provides insight on collective action and support at a key life-course phase for women. She explores how women talk about the menopause and how they develop strategies to explain, account and cope. Stephens explores the impact of motherhood on the lives and experiences of professional medical women. She collected data which captured the decision making processes and everyday realities associated with their dual roles and 'careers'; as doctor and mother. Parsons interviewed mothers and daughters in families known to be carriers of the Duchenne Muscular Dystrophy gene. She explores their generational relationships and decisions about parenthood. All three of these chapters place the life course, and key moments of life course transition, as central to the lives and experiences of women.

All of the chapters in this volume draw on detailed empirical research with the exception of Adam. This chapter does not at first glance fit into an edited collection on empirical qualitative work on gender. We have included this chapter because it makes an important contribution to the work on gender which is located at Cardiff. The theoretical perspectives which Adam outlines are not necessarily theories to which any of our contributors have directly referred. However the empirical work on gender which is presented in this volume has benefited from a lively theoretical culture as well as the strong qualitative research culture which is to be found at Cardiff. Most of the chapters in this volume adopt a broadly interactionist approach and are strongly located in the empirical. But they are all informed by broader theoretical and epistemological perspectives, of which the work of Adam is particularly pertinent.

# 1  Masculinity in prison

*Keith Carter*

This chapter discusses the construction and display of masculinity in a local prison in the United Kingdom. This is a predominantly male institutional environment where only four women prison officers work. It is argued that the men (inmates and staff) inside the prison highly prize and use their 'manliness' to establish and maintain self esteem, meaning and power. For inmates who are doing time (Cohen and Taylor, 1972) or staff who are serving time (Carter, 1995), everyday life in the prison depends on the ability to survive the pains of imprisonment (Sykes, 1958). The expression of masculinity is an essential survival strategy for staff and inmates alike. Such survival means getting through the day with 'easy time': with the least possible hassle. For all the institutional differences between staff and inmates, they share a common gender identity, similar educational experiences, and working class origins. They share a culture of strong language, humour and stereotyped ideas of maleness. Such cultural idioms are used continually by both the groups in negotiating easy time and personal respect.

**Locating the research**

The chapter draws on eighteen months of ethnographic fieldwork, examining the occupational culture of prison officers. Methods employed (observations, unstructured interviews, and a questionnaire to staff) were aimed at documenting the experiences, feelings and working practices of the uniformed staff and how they made sense of their world. I had unrestricted access throughout the whole prison, with my own set of keys. It is the first sociological study of prison officers since the study by Morris and Morris (1963) at Pentonville.

The prison is referred to by the pseudonym 'Martindale'. All social actors within the setting are also given pseudonyms. Martindale is a local Victorian prison located within the boundary of a medium-sized city. As a local prison, it houses a cross section of male offenders drawn from the immediate geographical area. Martindale acts as a holding site for offenders from the point of arrest until conviction. Once convicted, prisoners are usually transferred to other establishments. Because the prison holds offenders of all types, the prison population at Martindale is a highly volatile and transient one.

The prison officers who work at Martindale are also drawn from the local geographical area, and in the majority of cases share with inmates a working-class background and local ties (cf. Morris and Morris, 1963; Thomas, 1972; Fleischer, 1989; Kauffman, 1988; Lombardo, 1989; Carter, 1994). At Martindale it is not unknown for prisoners and prison officers to come from the same neighbourhood, to have attended the same school, to have mutual acquaintances and shared experiences. At the time of research Martindale had only four women prison officers out of around 200 male staff. Martindale is thus embedded in, and reflects, a local male working class culture.

**Masculinity and the prison setting**

Gender was not in itself the primary analytic focus of my ethnography of Martindale. However, it proved to be fundamental in understanding the prison regime, not least by virtue of the homogeneity of gender identities to be found there. Prisons do not have the social diversity found in the outside world because they are socially excluded from that world. Outside the prison setting, masculinity is complex, multidimensional and experienced differently within a myriad of changing and different cultural, historical and social locations (see Mac an Ghaill, 1995; Connell, 1995).

If, as Edley and Wetherell (1995) argue, masculinity is the sum of men's characteristics; at work, with their families, in groups and institutions, then masculinity in the prison is one-dimensional. Inside Martindale there are no families, no permitted sexual relationships, no workplace (in comparison with the outside), no gender balanced home or community. What is left are institutional male groups of staff and inmates. In the absence of a diversity of social relationships the men draw on a common stock of understandings about masculinity, and institutional modes of expression.

Much of the contemporary literature and criminological research on masculinity refers to gender and violence (Hall *et al.*, 1978; Stanko, 1990;

Liddle, 1993; Messerschmidt, 1994; Scully, 1989; Dobash and Dobash, 1992). Issues of masculinity in Martindale were not restricted to problems of criminal violence, however. Some of the inmates did have records of serious violence, but such behaviour is rare inside the prison. The prisoners used other means to express their masculine identity. In the rest of the chapter I discuss some of those strategies: displays of composure, strength and physical control; the exercise of power and bargaining skills; ritual combat and linguistic display.

### Composure, strength and physical control

Research has shown that men are often reluctant to admit to vunerability or fear (Stanko and Hobdell 1993). Many of the staff and inmates at Martindale would not admit to each other that they were frightened (although they might have admitted it to a researcher outside the hearing of their colleagues). Prison officers viewed requests for help from colleagues to betray professional weakness. There was an implicit understanding that asking for help was tantamount to admitting that you were not man enough to do the job. Officers must always appear to be strong and able to deal effectively with all eventualities. Asking for help, showing fear or emotion is not occupationally acceptable. Prison Officer Read told me,

> When I transferred here I really felt vulnerable because no one told me what to do. There's no support, you just get on with the job. I remember going home and just crying to my wife. You cannot do that in prison.

This was typical of prison officers expressions of occupational culture. On numerous occasions I was told 'you have to be in charge'; 'take no shit from them'; 'it's really about being a man'. Criticising a fellow member of staff, Prison Officer Hall said,

> We call him the 'mouse' because he's frightened of the cons. He's no fucking use in a fight. I don't know how he got the job as a prison officer.

A similar criticism was made of the new prison governor by Prison Officer Church,

What do you think of the new governor? He's like a fucking weed. If he expects to lead a group of men he's got no chance.

Staff themselves had a clear picture of the personal qualities needed for working inside prison - physical strength and a 'manly' appearance (Cohen and Taylor, 1972; Carter, 1995). Prisoners also paraded their physical strength in front of the prison officers and other inmates. Many of them were active body builders and appeared to earn respect through their muscular appearance, and potential strength. Prison Officer Dodd said,

> Look at that bloke, he's built like a brick shit house. He's here on three charges of rape, but he's not Rule 43 [Vulnerable Prisoner Unit], he can cope with anything - no one will give him a hard time.

A muscular physique is a source of respect. It conveys to others the message to 'leave well alone'. Not all inmates look muscular and many of them who were not believed the best strategy was to keep their distance from the more physically powerful.

The value attached to physical strength is matched by the need to display emotional control. The expression of emotion may be taken for weakness. A prisoner remarked, about domestic visits,

> It's better not to show that you're upset to the family, it only adds to their worries. I try to put on a show so my wife does not worry about me. What's the point if we both end up crying in front of all those bastards. You cannot say what you want inside visits.

Inmates attempted to hide from prison staff and other prisoners what could be construed as a gentler side. They believed that showing any kind of 'soft' emotion was dangerous. Like the Government Health Warning advertisement on cigarettes, one inmate remarked to me,

> The Health Warning here is keep to yourself and be distant. Being open or too caring can be injurious to your health.

When we were alone, another prisoner told me:

> Keith, here I keep myself to myself. It's no use being gentle
> or too friendly in a place like this. Someone might take it
> the wrong way. You've got to be a man's man.

Inside Martindale being seen as a 'man's man' was a central survival strategy for staff and inmates. The concept of being a man's man is linked to traditional male gender stereotypes of strength, aggression and individualism (Archer and Lloyd, 1985). Both groups therefore engaged in public displays of physical and emotional strength, while hiding private fears and weaknesses. Edley and Wetherall (1995, p.211) argue that 'men choose their masculinity but only within the confines of the menu'. Prison menus are limited. Variety is perceived as dangerous; behaviour that strays from restricted norms of masculinity is institutionally unacceptable. Masculinity in prison is not a private identity, but is institutionally framed by publicly observable action. What counts as being a man inside Martindale is limited to those institutionally defined codes of conduct and comportment. The local norms of strength and control impose a restricted set of available definitions of acceptable masculine identity.

**Power and bargaining skills**

For the men in Martindale, masculinity was essential to their everyday survival. This in turn, was linked to processes of bargaining, negotiation and control. For the prison officers, this depended upon their ability to exercise control over prisoners. This reflects more general orientations towards work and the problematic nature of control. Edley and Wetherell (1995, p.103) argue that:

> work can ... be a place where men act out a macho sense of
> being proper men, validating this identity through various
> male fraternities. Yet for many working-class men, work has
> become an experience of powerlessness, of inter-
> changeability with others, of redundancy, an experience of
> humiliation through subordination to authority.

Many of the prison officers believed that their power to control inmates had been eroded over the last fifty years or so, by several elements. The pressures of overcrowding, new prison routines and new competing managerial ideologies were felt to have undermined the exercise of control. This is not restricted to Martindale, but reflects wider changes in prison policy and practice (Home Office, 1987; Woolf, 1991; Senese, 1994). These have also resulted in new liberal regimes and personal freedoms inside the prison - increased association, more visiting privileges and access to telephones. Many of these changes have empowered the inmates and reduced the power of the staff over them (see Woolf, 1991). Many of the prison officers at Martindale believed that their power to control inmates had not only been eroded by the liberalisation of prison regimes. The organization of prison officers' work regimes was also pointed to. At Martindale there was an apparent lack of any cohesive and systematic supervision of landing officers (basic grade staff who work with the inmates on the wings). This was matched by a lack of organized solidarity among the staff. The lack of directive supervision allowed each officer to interpret the prison rules individually. The consequence was a loss of collective power. This lack of control made some of them, at times, fear for their own safety and feel inadequate. They felt less masculine. Prison Officer Carole stated that,

> After the riots, we all worked together. It was a tight ship
> and the cons knew where they stood. We were together.
> Now every officer does what he wants. If a con cannot get it
> from me he just goes somewhere else.

During normal working periods, when there are no serious disturbances or riots, there is only a minimum number of officers in the prison to supervise the inmates, and the emphasis towards strict security is diluted. At these times, each officer interprets the rules and regulations on an individual basis and there appears to be no internal group solidarity amongst the staff. Group power has dissolved at Martindale. As Arendt (1970, p.44) suggests:

> Power is never the property of an individual; it belongs to a
> group and remains in existence only so long as the group
> keeps together. When we say of somebody, that he is 'in
> power' we actually refer to his being empowered by a certain
> number of people to act in their name. The moment the
> group, from which the power originated to begin with
> (*potestas in populo*, without a people or groups there is no
> power), disappears, 'his power' also vanishes.

Group power to control inmates at Martindale had been diluted and marginalised by inconsistent and individualistic working practices, the lack of a corporate policy and the lack of supervision by some of the staff. As a result, the control of inmates was like a see-saw, operating rigidly only in times of serious disturbance or riot situations. In times of 'normality', which is the vast majority of time, the prisoners were able to exercise considerable influence over the officers' capacity to control the prison.

In practice there was a great deal of bargaining between individuals. Individualistic treatment of prisoners was tacitly condoned as long as it did not disrupt the internal prison routines. Equally, such treatment should not threaten the status of the officer in the eyes of his colleagues or inmates. Such condoned deviation from normal practice was often of a token nature. One example of such behaviour would be granting permission to an inmate who wants to shower in other than during his allotted time. The request may be allowed if there are sufficient prison officers, or the shower would not affect the normal routines, or the officer would not be seen by the other cons or his colleagues, as a 'soft touch', 'weak', or favouring the inmate, and thus less of a man's man. The dilemma facing some staff working in such close proximity is elucidated by Officer King:

> If you allow one to buck the system then they all want it. If you allow one to get away with it then how can I say no to another. Giving them extras just causes extra friction and problems.

Thomas (1978, p.55) suggests that prison staff have two ways to enforce conformity amongst prisoners, naked force and a reward system. The first option is rarely used in Martindale; the second is used as a powerful incentive to encourage conformity.

Some of Martindale's officers believed that in the face of reduced institutional power, they had to achieve personal 'manliness' by less formal means. It was no longer enough to direct, order, or cajole some of their captives to obey the rules. The rules themselves had to be legitimated and at times altered by the staff before some of the prisoners would conform to them. Prison Officer Hall put it like this,

> I wouldn't expect a con to shower only once a week. That rule is stupid and there's no way I could justify it. If he wants a shower then good luck to him. The con over there understands the fair way I treat him so if I told him to get in his cell he wouldn't argue with me. You have to give and take here.

Prison officers, in a sense, 'barter' with inmates for compliance by allowing them extras. These can be in the form of extra tobacco, the use of telephones, extra time in visits, showers, extra pillows, gas lighters and so forth. These extra privileges were usually given to 'OK cons' who were not seen as security or control problems to the staff. By conforming to the rules and showing respect to the prison officers (doing as they are told) many of the inmates secured better treatment. In return, the prison officers could obtain overt respect and the validation of their masculine identity.

**Ritual combat and linguistic display**

Where staff have a monopoly on the official power, autonomy and control inside a relatively closed environment, the inmates are likely to challenge their authority. Inevitably, therefore, arguments in Martindale were commonplace. Both groups were looking for respect from each other. In this male dominated society, self-esteem, masculinity and respect were highly prized. Officers and prisoners engaged in games or forms of ritual combat, in order to challenge one another. The 'captives and the captors' (Sykes, 1958), had developed a working relationship, based on challenges and games. Played out between grown men, but very similar to the games small boys play, such as, Cowboys and Indians, Cops and Robbers, or Soldiers, but without the imitation weapons. With no weapons, apart from their own male persona, each group attempted to dissolve and challenge the power of the other, by the use of wit, threat and subterfuge. This is somewhat similar to the male police culture where, 'combat with villains is a ritualised game, ... a fun challenge with winning by arrest' (Reiner, 1993, p.113).

Just as the police officer can ensure victory through an arrest, prison officers can win the game by reporting an inmate for an offence. But the main satisfaction is gained from the act of catching out an offender, not the official report or the consequent sanctions. For the prisoner's personal status is thus weakened. It is a game of small victories on both sides: one group, 'the captors', attempt to impose control under the guise of security, whilst 'the captives' are always attempting to gain more freedom, extra privileges, independence and more autonomy. Both groups see their masculinity as inextricably linked to the power they wield over the other. One inmate remarked,

> I play the game, lick their arses. If they shout and swear I
> just laugh it off. That's the way you get better treatment, and

an easier time. If you fight back, or buck the system and argue, you lose your job. So it's best to pretend to play their game.

Such game-playing is seen by some of the prisoners as a way of gaining self-esteem, or fighting back against the system. Challenging the authority of the officers and openly baiting them, especially when there are other inmates about, or when the staff are outnumbered, are common strategies of ritualised resistance.

Searches for prohibited property provide the occasion for such ritualised exchanges. The inmates are aware that some officers are very vigilant; always attempting to catch them with unauthorised property, such as drugs, prohibited lighters, cash, stolen property from within the prison, extra bedding, pillows, sheets or even alcohol kits (plastic containers and fermenting fruit, used to make alcohol). For instance, one officer, engaged in cell-searching, found a piece of toilet paper, wrapped up and hidden, in the corner of an inmate cell. The officer opened it and laughed out loud. Written on the paper were the words, 'Not quite there you bastards, but you're getting warmer'. The officer remarked:

> I know he's been smoking whacky baccy (cannabis), but you have got to give him credit for cheek. I'll catch him eventually.

In another cell officers found a Prison Department official notice board, about two feet by three feet in size. It contained the words in very large letters, *'NO INMATE IS ALLOWED TO REMOVE ANY ARTICLE WITHOUT PERMISSION'*. This sign had been taken by an inmate, carried concealed through the prison, under the eyes of all the staff on duty and successfully hidden in his cell. There was no purpose in possessing it, apart from 'beating the bastards'. There is thus a game of cat-and-mouse played out around such actions.

Officers are well aware that inmates break the rules, especially on domestic visits. There is little they can do after the event, but they make sure that the inmate is under no illusions about the incident. For example, on one occasion in the searching area, a room used for searching prisoners after they have left their visitors, a searcher (prison officer) said to a prisoner, 'Phew! Don't breath on me', waving his hands in front of his mouth, and smiling at the same time. The inmate with a beaming smile across his face said, 'Okay Boss, I'll be sensible. I won't cause any trouble'. The prisoner had been drinking whisky during visits. Although the officer could not do anything after the event, he still wanted to make sure that the incident did not go un-noticed. Another member of staff, searching after visits, saw an inmate hide a gas lighter inside his shoe. When the officer asked to see the shoes the inmate transferred the lighter into his hand. The officer said quietly, winking his eye, 'You'll have to be better than that to have one over me'. The officer told me later that he could have 'nicked him for it' but by catching him he had 'won the game'. The possession of a gas lighter, in his estimation, could be allowed to certain, trustworthy inmates, because they were 'Okay cons', causing no problems. The main message in this exchange between the 'captor' and the 'captive', was the 'captor' still retained his power and authority.

Linguistic displays are also used in the ritualised contest of the prison. Arguments, shouting and verbal abuse are generally directed by prisoners towards particular officers, or the prison system as a whole. The fabric of the prison lends itself to noise. Arguments reverberate around the wings and landings, informing both the staff and inmates of potential trouble. Arguments tend to be individual incidents, between one officer and one inmate. It is, however, extremely difficult to conceal them or keep them private. Apparent private disputes therefore convey more public messages. In the course of these exchanges, staff and prisoners use very strong language. As has already been suggested, the culture of the prison reflects an ethos of working-class masculinity (Kauffman, 1988; Lombardo, 1989; Fleischer, 1988; Thomas, 1978; Carter, 1994). The subculture of the prison, including its language, is 'imported' into the institution (Hawkins, 1976) by both the staff and inmates. It is, therefore, characteristic of this culture that prisoners and prison officers use highly graphic and strongly sexist language. Inmates are well aware of what they can get away with. The message game is to push or challenge the staff, and the inmates as far as they can, without provoking reprisals. Making your opponent feel less of a man in front of his peers reinforces your own status as a man.

Inmates realise that there is little staff can do about insulting behaviour, or bad language. Both groups adopt similar insulting or demeaning linguistic strategies when dealing with each other. It is rarely challenged formally. Even when the bad language is directed personally against an officer or an inmate, formal complaint rarely occurs. Whilst it is acknowledged that the staff can take formal action more readily than the inmates, many of them believe that such action is unnecessary. Prison Officer Dodd, for instance, argued that making it official could give the impression that he lacked strength of character; wasn't man enough to do the job:

> I don't need Big Brother to help me sort out a landing. I'm man enough to do it myself. If I took action against someone for insulting me, it would appear I cannot control them. Here we give as good as we get. They slag you off so I do the same. They understand it better if you throw a few fucks into them.

Being man enough to deal with the problem and to take the verbal abuse alone shows to others (staff and inmates) that you have the necessary strength, respect and manliness to do the job.

'Slagging off' or demeaning staff in front of other inmates and their colleagues is done openly as an act of male bravado, an open challenge to their masculinity, power and authority. The louder the exchange of insults, the greater the message to other staff and inmates that this prisoner still has rights and no one should mess with him For example, during one cell search (staff search inmates' cells for stolen property, drugs and examine the locks, bolts and bars for security reasons), when about 20 inmates were congregated on the same landing, a prisoner shouted at one of the officers standing outside his cell,

> Fucking cunt, why pick on us you bastards? I'll speak to him [researcher], he looks important so you can fuck off.

Another inmate shouted at a member of staff searching his cell, 'You load of cunts, get out of my cell'. In every incident of this sort, the statements were directed to the officers personally, but the prisoners were also acting to a greater audience. Inmates were well aware that there was little that the officers could do about their behaviour, because they were outnumbered and this was no time to use force. If action were to be taken it would be later, when sufficient staff were available to deal effectively with any incident.

Just as the officers rarely report insulting language, inmates are also dissuaded from complaining to higher authority about verbal abuse directed at them. They risk losing their prison jobs or any extra privileges if they report an officer for being insulting. Many feel that it's just not worth the trouble, and they are reluctant to 'buck the system'. Each group is therefore reluctant to report the behaviour officially: it is generally forgotten, or 'put on the tab' for another time. When complaints *are* made, prisoners and staff stick together.

The game of verbal abuse is played by both sides, but the staff interpret the boundaries of acceptable behaviour. The abuse used by many of the staff is hidden, under an umbrella of institutional humour, and considered 'normal banter'. Drummond (1992, p.138) has noted how American prisoners use abusive language including highly sexualized terms such as 'gorilla', 'daddy', 'kid', 'fag' and 'queen', which become 'sexual scripts which help to define an inmate's orientation within a society which values aggression, power and loyalty - many of the attributes of traditional masculinity in society'. Prison officers at Martindale use similar epithets, including sexualized terms, openly calling the inmates dick-heads, shits, cunts, cheeky bastards, and wankers. At times the inmates replied in the same terms. This kind of exchange is a normal part of the macho prison culture. Stanko (1990, pp.123-4) notes that,

> Inmate power and control can be gained by treating other inmates 'like women', essentially keeping the fear of sexual danger associated with being a female. By turning some men into 'women' these inmates use sexuality to dehumanise and degrade fellow inmates.

The inmates at Martindale not only degrade each other, they also degrade the staff. A number of officers, after being insulted by inmates, said they felt embarrassed because they were 'made to look like a cunt in front of the cons'. Calling officers the names of female genitalia, was highly insulting to some staff. It was felt as a direct challenge to their masculinity, an open threat to their personal authority and disrespectful. This loss of face inside the total institution is difficult for many officers to take, especially when the inmate has openly challenged their manhood, or verbally 'castrated' them (see Edley and Wetherell, 1995). When inmates become too disrespectful, some of the staff believe that a more forceful approach is needed to 'teach them a lesson.' Prison Officer Hall said; 'I'll wait my time, they need you more than you need them. Just wait till he wants something. He'll get fuck all'.

Prison officers who had been made to feel like women, in front of the cons, exacted their own retribution, either officially or unofficially. One officer slapped a prisoner when searching him saying; 'Don't you ever make me look a cunt in front of the cons you bastard. Do you understand'. Another officer had previously been insulted by an inmate in front of the other prisoners and his colleagues. Coming off a control and research team where force had been used he said; 'I chose the guy who I was going to have. I've waited six months for that bastard. I knew I would get my own back.

Whilst some prison officers do openly admit to 'getting their own back' many of the staff at Martindale are not so open. They are however, all concerned about how others see them; being 'male' demands respect from all quarters. Respect is a integral part of masculine culture found in Martindale.

## Conclusion

All the male social actors at Martindale, prisoners and staff, attempt to deceive each other. They cling to what they consider to be the essential characteristics of 'traditional' maleness. They act out to each other, and to their peers, a masculine code of conduct. This involves being seen as physically and mentally strong, well able to cope, aggressive and always in control. On their own (out of view of their peers) they display other emotions, such as fear, tenderness, caring and concern for others, but the system prevents them from showing that side of their character or 'coming out' to others. The risk of being taken advantage of by other men, and thus losing face, inside a male dominated environment, is too great.

Both groups share common social backgrounds and beliefs of what they regard as 'maleness'. From their different positions within the institution they play out these beliefs to each other. What they are both looking for, from each other and their peers, is personal respect and self-esteem. Many of them attempt to achieve their masculinity by being 'strong at all times', aggressive; above all in charge of their own spatially restricted world. Arguments, strong language and the games played between these groups help to reinforce their self-esteem.

A common strategy of challenging masculinity is to reduce the opponent to the role of a woman in front of other men. This verbal de-masculisation is, in a sense, a public denial of maleness. Prisons are not places which build self-esteem. Asking for simple items such as toilet paper, a razor, soap, a letter, or clean underclothes does not build up esteem. On the contrary, it degrades it. Inmates resort to verbal abuse and any other strategy, apart from physical force, in order to regain some of their lost status.

The display of masculine identity within the prison setting is intimately tied up with the power relationships between staff and inmates. Through a variety of strategies, the men attempt to demonstrate their masculinity and the values which they associate with it. This chapter has shown that those strategies are common to both officers and prisons. Masculinity inside the prison setting is both shared and negotiated.

The observations and interpretations contained in this chapter may well have been influenced by my own gender and my own feelings of powerlessness. There is no doubt that my own occupational socialisation as a police officer, together with my working class background and my status as a postgraduate student influenced what I saw and how I saw it. They may to some extent have influenced the research questions I asked. Another researcher of a different gender, age, or social background may well have seen things differently or reached different conclusions. As Catherine Kauffman (1988 p.277), rightly, points out,

> More is learnt from a collage than from a single photograph, an argument not only for more research, but also for a diversity among researchers.

## References

Archer and Lloyd (1985), (eds) *Sex and gender*, Cambridge, Cambridge University Press.

Arendt, H. (1970), *On violence.* London, Allen Lane.

Carter, K. (1994), 'Prison officers and their survival strategies', in *Occupational socialisation and working lives.* (eds) Coffey, A. and Atkinson, P. Avebury, London, pp.41-57.

Carter, K. (1995), *The occupational socialisation of prison officers: an ethnography.* Unpublished Phd, University Of Wales, Cardiff.

Cohen, S. and Taylor, L. (1972), *Psychological survival - the experience of long term imprisonment.* Harmonsworth, Middlesex, Penguin Books.

Connell, R. (1987), *Gender and power.* Cambridge, Polity Press.

Connell, R. (1995), *Masculinities,* Cambridge, Polity Press.

Dobash, R. and Dobash, R (1992), *Women, violence and social change.* London, Routledge.

Drummond, R. (1992), in Newburn , T and Stanko, E. (eds) (1994), *Just boys doing the business.* London, Routledge, pp.48-67.

Edley, N. and Wetherell, M. (1995), *Men in perspective, practice, power and identity.* London, Prentice Hall Harvester, Wheatsheaf.

Fleischer, M. (1989), *Warehousing violence.* London, Sage Publications.

Mac an Ghaill, M. (ed.) (1995), *Understanding masculinities: social relations and cultural areas.* Open University Press, Milton Keynes.

Hall, S., Critcher, C., Jefferson, T. and Roberts, B. (1978), *Policing the crisis*. London, Macmillan.

Hawkins, G. (1976), *The prison; policy and practice*. Chicago, University of Chicago Press.

Home Office (1987), *A fresh start - Bulletin No 8*. London, Central Office for Information. London: HMSO

Kauffman, K. (1988), *Prison officers and their world.* Cambridge, Massachusetts, Harvard University Press.

Liddle, M. (1993), 'Masculinity, 'male behaviour' and crime: a theoretical investigation of sex-differences in delinquency and deviant behaviour' in E. Stanko (ed.) *Masculinity and crime: issues of theory and practice:* Conference report. Centre for Criminal Justice Research, Brunel The University of West London, September, 1993.

Lombardo, L. (1989), *Guards imprisoned: correctional officers at work second edition.* Cincinnati, OH, Anderson Publishing Company.

Messerschmidt, J. (1993), *Masculinities and crime: critique and reconceptualization of theory.* Maryland, Rowman and Littlefield.

Morris, T. and Morris P. (1963), *Pentonville - a sociological study of an English prison*, London, Routledge and Kegan Paul Ltd.

Reiner, R. (1993), *Politics of police* (2nd edition). Brighton, Wheatsheaf.

Scully, D. (1990), *Understanding sexual violence: a study of convicted rapists.* London, Harper Collins.

Senese, J. (1994), Control in prisons: a*n assessment of the use of force in American prisons.* Paper presented at Prisons 2000 An International Conference on the Present State and Future of the Prison System. Centre for Public Order: Imprisonment, University of Leicester. England. April 1994.

Sim, J. (1994), 'Tougher than the rest? Men in Prison' in Newburn, T. and Stanko, B (eds) *Just boys doing the business.* London, Routledge, pp.74-90.

Stanko, A. (1990), *Everyday violence.* London, Pandora.

Stanko, A. and Hobdell, K. (1993), 'Assault on men: masculinity and male victimization' *British Journal of Criminology.* Vol 33 Summer 1993 p.400-415.

Sykes, G. (1958), *The society of captives: a study of a maximum security prison*, Princeton, New Jersey, Princeton University Press.

Thomas, J. (1978), A good man for gaoler? - Crisis discontent and the prison staff in Freeman, J (ed.) *Prison past and future.* London, Heinemann, pp.56-72.

Thomas, J. (1972), *The English prison officer since 1850.* London, Routledge & Kegan Paul Ltd.

Woolf Report (1991), *Prison disturbances April 1990.* London, HMSO.

# 2 Coping with pit closure in the 1990s: Women's perspectives

*Bella Dicks*

**Introduction**

In October 1992, Michael Hesletine announced the sweeping round of pit closures that was subsequently to signal the virtual elimination of Britain's deep coal-mining tradition. The ensuing public outcry in the media focused heavily on the consequent social destruction awaiting scores of mining communities. Inevitably, perhaps, the media campaign focused mainly on the social disintegration occasioned by male job loss: the loss of community 'pride' in the wake of male redundancy, and the loss of the community's 'heart' with the closure of the colliery. The underlying assumption was that the problems of a locally-situated people flow from the loss of the family wage and from the loss of locally-based male employment. The following observations are intended to fill in some missing dimensions from this skeletal picture, particularly concerning the position of women in areas which have long afforded them few employment opportunities. Far from being launched into a sudden and localised decline, families in coalfield communities have been coping with the effects of wider de-industrialisation and restructuring at least since the 1970s, and women have suffered in parallel ways to men. Their own labour-market experiences and their own mediated responses to spouse redundancy are the subject of this chapter, which presents material from a two-year study of four mining communities in South Yorkshire.

Since my concern here is to highlight issues concerning the experiences of women after pit closure, I focus on two of the communities studied, which, at the time of fieldwork, had already lost their local colliery. The closures resulted in the loss of the only major source of local employment for men, and in both cases took the official male unemployment rate above 23 percent. However, what I document here is how the women in our interview sample experienced this fundamental change in the local community, and how the onset of male redundancy interacted with other factors in their lives (such as their own employment, domestic role and local social networks). The 18 women interviewed in these two communities were all the partners of miners or ex-miners from the local pit (who were currently unemployed, transferred to a different colliery, or re-employed outside the mining industry). The major focus of this chapter will be on those women with unemployed partners: our survey of 200 miners and their partners across the two communities indicated that around half of ex-miners remained unemployed 18 months after pit closure (Waddington, Dicks and Critcher, 1994). I shall also consider the experiences of women whose partners had found alternative employment, in order to explore some of the issues of the 'post-mining household'. Finally, I offer some insights into the labour market position of women: in low-paid service sector jobs that were all the local economy could offer. Women, as well as men, were facing insecure employment futures.

The data drawn on in this chapter are taken from a wider pool of 30 in-depth, semi-structured interviews carried out by myself during the Summer of 1992 in four mining communities. A similar number of interviews with men were also completed. The research was designed to combine both quantitative and qualitative methods in a two-stage process; face-to-face administered questionnaires followed by in-depth taperecorded interviews with a smaller sub-set. The interview sample was selected from a data base of 480 ex-miners, miners and their partners from the four communities, compiled by the research team from the questionnaire-based survey carried out the previous year. Interviewees were selected according to age, employment status of self and partner, and level of stress (measured using a version of the General Health Questionnaire). Interview schedules were designed to find out what, if any, the pressure points were in women's lives; how they viewed the local community and its support networks; and how their partners were responding to redundancy or re-employment. The in-depth, two-hour interviews were able to evidence the complexity of factors affecting women's well-being, and both supplement and in many cases re-define, the survey findings. What emerged from these data, was that women's ability to cope with the aftermath of pit closure is not decided so much by their spouses' employment fate as by the material, social and emotional resources that women can claim for themselves within the restraints of a cultural context of unequal gender relations.

The restructuring of the British economy and the accompanying de-industrialisation of many urban areas, particularly in the North of England (but also in South Wales and parts of the Midlands), has been extensively analysed and documented (see Massey, 1984; Bagguley *et. al.*, 1990, Allen, and Massey, 1988). It is a phenomenon that has produced stubbornly high levels of unemployment in Britain's older industrial centres, which have lasted more than a decade. The accompanying far-reaching ramifications on social life and, in particular, on domestic and labour-market relations have generated a substantial body of sociological work. In the early and mid 1980s an important strand of this work concentrated on the effects of unemployment on individuals and families - a research tradition which was, from the start, characterised by an emphasis on the importance of gender dimensions in unemployment and its effects (Martin and Wallace, 1984; Fagin and Little, 1984; Popay, 1985), as well as by an older tradition that privileged class-based and economistic explanations. Interest in unemployment has perhaps fallen away somewhat in the 1990s, as other agendas in academic research have come to the fore. Nevertheless, some of the themes of the earlier work can usefully be re-addressed in the current climate. Endemic unemployment remains a persistent feature in the UK's 'spatial divisions of labour', and the relative position of men and women with regard to employment access is still a high-profile issue. In addition, with many media commentators arguing that there is a specifically gendered (i.e. masculinist) dimension to the problems of the so-called 'underclass' in Britain's ex-industrial communities (Campbell, 1993), it seems that the study of both men's and women's responses to unemployment is more pertinent than ever.

The 1980s studies demonstrated that the social and psychological effects of unemployment impacted not only upon the unemployed individuals themselves, but on members of their families, and on extended kinship and social networks (McKee and Bell, 1985; Jackson and Walsh, 1987). This research tradition has insisted on recognition of the fact that unemployed men were not merely part of the 'reserve army of labour', as in class-based analyses, but were also part of social formations such as the household and the family, with their own particular (patriarchal) structures. Since women remained largely responsible for household management and childcare, the tasks of budgeting and catering on a reduced income, as well as the provision of emotional support to distressed partners, largely fell on their shoulders. In this sense, male unemployment constituted a burden that women were disproportionately required to carry. We could say, therefore, that women have been seen as victims of male unemployment, particularly as the hypothesis of a reversal of the domestic division of labour received scant support from empirical studies (Pahl, 1984; Morris, 1985; Laite and Halfpenny, 1987; though see also Wheelock, 1990 and Gallie *et. al.* 1993 on the evidence of modest change).

Although this concern to widen the field of unemployment effects from the individual to the household is certainly justified and indeed essential, there is a danger that women emerge from this type of study as the rather passive recipients of stress initiated by the labour market experiences of men. This results partly from the tendency to separate studies of the household that examine the effects of male job loss (for example McKee and Bell, 1985, 1986), from studies that examine the question of women's own redundancy (for example Coyle, 1984). In what follows, I present data on women's experiences in the wake of pit closure that approach the question of women's stress from a more holistic perspective. The interview data indicate a range of different factors that mediate the fact of pit closure and the onset of male redundancy for women. These are manifested both within women's 'horizontal' (i.e. inter-personal) relationship to their spouse and their families, but also their own 'vertical' (i.e. institutional) relationship to the local labour market. In order to map the problems that women face in Britain's ex-mining communities, we need to recognise that women's stress is not merely a function of their partners' job loss. Indeed, the gradual run-down and final closure of the pit is accompanied by shifts in all aspects of the local labour market and the identity of the community. Women have their own independent relation to these structural stressors. Men's and women's lives are touched in distinct yet parallel ways by these changes.

The first part of this chapter looks at the nature of the ramifications for women of spouse redundancy, and thus continues the tradition of studying unemployment in the context of the household. This section is concerned with the problems directly occasioned for women by the loss of their partners' employment. I then broaden the discussion further by looking at how pit closure also impacts upon women's own independent relation to the local labour market. It is therefore concerned with the problems occasioned for women by economic restructuring in general. Throughout, my emphasis will be on the social and psychological effects of structural change: the material and financial aspects, although important, are ones that I will not have space to cover.

**Male unemployment: conflict over the breadwinner identity and the domestic division of labour**

Where attention is confined to women's responses to a partner's redundancy, the question of women's own employment remains a crucial element in the extent to which this redundancy becomes problematic. In what follows I map out the complex interplay of women's own employment situation, and that of her partner, in the production of stress. Both of these external forces, which meet at the intersection of women's personal lives, are played out within a framework of microcosmic gender relations. Where there is severe strain imposed by these forces, it is the domestic division of labour that becomes the primary site of struggle. This can have the effect of problematising women's access to paid work outside of the home. For example, one of the observable effects of spouse redundancy that women experienced is the onset of irritability, bitterness and anger on the part of their unemployed partners as the prospect of quickly finding re-employment recedes. This is particularly exacerbated in the case of mining, where redundancy has almost always been preceded by a lengthy period of uncertainty and struggle over pit closure, and by a process of difficult decision-making for the ex-miner over whether to opt for a transfer or for the redundancy package. However this irritability is always framed within the gender power relations of the couple, and as such is not merely a personal psychological response to job loss. Instead, it means that the question of women's own access to employment frequently becomes a site of contestation, as the traditional cultural reliance on the male breadwinner role is successively eroded.

Male frustration over unemployment was manifested in different ways in my interview sample. While some women reported that their partners had become withdrawn and uncommunicative, others described their partners as irritable and short-tempered. Mrs M., for instance, whose husband had been unable to find work and bitterly regretted taking redundancy instead of a transfer, said he had become very depressed:

> He wishes now that he hadn't taken his redundancy, and I do too. He's right moody and temperamental now. He gets depressed. If he had his time again he'd have taken a transfer. He thought he'd have been able to get a job but it didn't turn out that way.

Their relationship had been severely affected: 'He's been very depressed, very argumentative. We used to have the odd argument but not like now. He just can't cope with not having a job'. Mrs. M.'s experiences were mirrored by other women in the sample with unemployed partners.

The extent to which women were having to cope with their partners' emotional reactions to redundancy is a clear indication of the strain that unemployment can impose on personal relationships. To interpret this simply as an instance of women carrying the burden of coping with their partners' anger and frustration, is to miss the significance of the content of such outbursts and heated exchanges. Almost inevitably, in the interview sample, these were centred on issues fundamentally bound up with struggle over gender identity and its symbolic content. In Mrs M.'s case, for example, her husband's anger and bad-temper were manifest in rows over her own continuation with her full-time employment as a care assistant, and over the couple's domestic division of labour. Her job had started to involve Mrs M. in leisure-time study for National Vocational Qualifications, and a perceived prospect of promotion, since her husband's unemployment began. Thus, at the very time when he was having to resign himself to joblessness, her work was beginning to assume the characteristics of a career - since it involved gaining qualifications, passing exams, and, crucially, now representing the only family wage. The couple had constant rows over her job. As she explained:

> He resented me working and fetching money in and him not having a job. He just felt as if he'd been a failure. It's hard to try and explain that he's kept me for 18 years and now I'm just doing my bit. He doesn't see it that way. He said, 'Pack the job in', and I said 'No'.

Rows were thus centred on her dual role as wage earner and housewife, and the question of her continuing in full-time work was inseparable from the issue of domestic labour:

> He used to think that housework was my job. If I couldn't do my job [in the house] and keep my job on at the same time, then he more or less said that I had to pack it in. That's what caused most of the rows... It really made me mad. I used to come in and think, 'I've just done a seven-hour shift, while he hasn't got up till 11 and he hasn't done a thing'. He hadn't hoovered up, there were no potatoes done, he wouldn't even go to the shops. I used to come in from work and he'd say 'You've no milk' or 'We need some bread'.

This response from her partner was a recent one, triggered specifically by his redundancy, since; 'on a normal day when he was still working at the pit, he'd come in and start helping to prepare the meal. After he'd finished at the pit, he just point blank refused to do anything. He wouldn't do a thing'. After 'eventually coming to a few blows' about this issue, Mrs M. gave her husband an ultimatum: either he accept the situation or the marriage was over. At the time of interview, they were in the immediate aftermath of this crisis; her husband was now participating to a limited extent in domestic labour. Now he would 'hoover up and wash the pots and go to the shops, which he never did before'. The threat of separation seemed to have receded, but Mrs M. stressed that she was still involved in an ongoing, gradual and difficult process of renegotiation with her husband.

The question of domestic conflict over women's access to paid work and responsibility for domestic labour is a complex and traumatic one. It immediately points to the way in which inter-personal responses to unemployment rest on deep-seated core tensions within traditional masculine and feminine identities. These turn on the breadwinner identity as a crucial masculine signifier. It is the loss of this symbolic power (as well as the material losses imposed by unemployment) and the loss of social networks and structured time that has frequently been observed to accompany prolonged unemployment (Jahoda, 1982), that forms the core of conflict and stress within the marital relationship. Women are thus not being passively acted on by male redundancy, but are launched into struggles around gender identity itself, in which they have to fight hard to hold on to positions that threaten to further deconstruct the masculine ideal. Appeals to 'rational' discourse, as in Mrs M's attempts to explain to her husband that 'he kept me for 18 years and now I'm just doing my bit' or to point out the financial impossibility of her giving up work, are potentially enfeebled in the face of these more powerful cultural assumptions.

The example presented above shows the ways in which inter-marital conflict can reverberate outside the particularities of the emotional relationship and become en-gendered through discourses of women's (and men's) wider social roles. Other types of inter-marital conflict also emerged in the interview data, which, although differently figured, can be seen as fissures in the edifice of the traditional gender division of labour. Struggles with partners over control and autonomy within domestic and leisure routines and schedules were frequently cited by women as major sources of stress. This subject was not explicitly addressed by the pre-prepared interview schedule, since it had been largely unanticipated. The frequency with which it was mentioned within a range of conversational contexts demonstrates the ways in which qualitative methods can yield insights that are too embedded for the question-specific stimulus-response framework of the questionnaire survey. Mrs P., for example, found that her unemployed husband resented her being absorbed in her own self-oriented leisure pursuits in the house during times that he felt were designated for relaxation:

> I get less time to relax now, because he doesn't like me sewing. I know he doesn't particularly like me doing it at night. Whereas before, I would sit, when he was on nights, every night until one o'clock in the morning if I wanted, I haven't done so as much since he's been out of work. So I don't get as much time to myself as before.

Mrs P. was experiencing the loss of her established routine and leisure patterns now that her husband had returned to the home full-time. Women had opportunities for autonomy and freedom of action within the home while the men had been employed for long hours at the pit, but these were threatened by mens' return to the home. This was especially the case for women, like Mrs P., who did not have access to extra-domestic autonomy through outside employment.

Other women experienced their unemployed husband's return to the home as a disruption of their own ownership of the domestic sphere. Mrs B.'s husband had expected to find other employment, but without success. Out of work for more than two years, he was finding unemployment very difficult to cope with, and his wife said that he had become 'moody and short-tempered'. Most importantly, he too, was now spending long periods of time in the house, which she described like this:

> I get fed-up at times. I know he can't help it. He's just sat there. He'll have a lie down, he'll do the garden, he goes to the job shop. I know it might sound selfish, but you can't get anything done. They're under your feet all the time. I can't do anything. I can't do what I want to do.

In this case, Mrs B. had few other spheres, other than that of her own nuclear family, in which to exercise autonomy and judgement. The question of her husband's literal dis-occupation was bound up with a new and unwelcome sense of her own.

This issue has frequently been noted in studies where women complain of unemployed partners 'getting under their feet' (McKee and Bell, 1985). This formulation of the problem tends to risk reducing its significance to a simple question of the daily annoyance caused by men impeding women's smooth-running domestic routines. However, it is important to take account of the deeper struggles over gender identity that this issue symbolises. For the first time in what was often a working career spanning twenty-five or thirty years, the onset of redundancy has deposited the man onto the domestic terrain *outside* of established 'leisure time'. Bostyn and Wight's

(1987) study of a Scottish ex-mining village emphasises the importance of the work-time/leisure-time dichotomy in traditional male-employed culture, and the persistence of this after unemployment. Previously, the 'being at home' versus 'being at work' opposition had, in most cases, structured men's sense of their role in the house in a particular way: they had been largely reactive, instead of pro-active, in the organisation of domestic routines, childcare and household labour. They were also used to seeing the home as a place of relaxation. Now, unemployment meant that the home had become their major sphere of activity and influence. In our interview sample the women reported a major qualitative shift in their experience of the 'housewife role' after male redundancy. For Mrs B., the constant presence of her husband represented a restriction on her freedom to organise her time in the house. What made this worse was the fact that his unemployment had coincided with the gradual disappearance of her own work outside the home, so that she had also lost access to independence from this source.

## Male unemployment: threats to women's own social networks and identity

The last section focused on the issue of marital conflict and sought to show how this was invariably framed within gendered parameters. However, not all of the women in the sample experienced spouse unemployment in terms of emotional strife. The following case study will present a different scenario, in which the onset of male redundancy occasions direct disruption to the woman's own extra-domestic identity, rather then being internalised within the interpersonal relationship. As other studies have shown (for example, Mattinson, 1988), marital problems may pre-exist unemployment, rather than simply be activated by its onset. The research presented here cannot offer evidence of this, but it seems likely that some partnerships are more able to withstand the effects of redundancy than others.

Mrs Br. reported that, like the other women we have discussed so far, her unemployed husband was finding it hard to cope with redundancy. However, she described his reactions as being fairly stoical:

> I don't even know if he's felt it yet to tell the truth. I don't know how long it takes. Once Johnny had left the pit, he'd left it and that was it. He said it was gone and that was it. I don't think he could bear to look on it, but he just said 'It's

gone and there's nothing I can do about it and I've got to move on'.

The fact that he had been offered a job, as a church worker in a different town, perhaps contributed to his resigned frame of mind, since he had an end to unemployment in sight. In any case, Mrs Br. did not find herself living with an irritable or short-tempered man giving vent to his frustrations. On the contrary, she described their relationship as very good: 'We laugh a lot. Maybe we haven't laughed as much recently but every now and then his sense of humour comes through'. What is significant about this relationship is that there was no apparent conflict over gender roles:

> I always felt that Johnny went out to work and earned the money and I did my job here and I did a good job. I was a wife and a mother, kept the house clean, had quite a few laughs with the family and why not? I'm a Christian so I believe that the husband should be the head of the house, so that I can rely on him.

However, this accepted and consciously-endorsed traditional division of labour was currently being destabilised - not by the spectre of role-reversal but by the couple's imminent move away to the new job and town. Mrs Br. had identified very strongly with the mining traditions of the community, and experienced the loss of the local pit as the loss of a family tradition and lineage:

> Although pit work is hard, that pit brought him up. His dad had worked there and we've lived on it. We were married when he was a miner. I married a miner and I'm proud of him, and I'm proud to be a miner's wife as well.

Previously, Mrs Br. had a strong sense of belonging in the community, but now she said 'I don't think there's any community spirit left', apart from among the 'old miners'. Furthermore, her involvement with the local church, which had not only provided her with a very close network of friends, but had also given her another identity outside the home - as a voluntary church bereavement counsellor - was to end with the move away. Through this work, she said she had gained independence and a sense of achievement; giving emotional support to a large number of people. She was now facing a double loss. Firstly, with the pit gone and the community changing, she felt that a whole set of traditions was disappearing. Secondly, the projected move was going to sever her links with her network of friends and neighbours and take away her counselling work. She expressed this as a disintegration of her whole way of life:

> He lost his job and then our son left home, and now our daughter's not coming with us. This house that we've put over 20 years into - we've done it up and enjoyed it because we've done it all together. I do a lot of voluntary work at the church and we'll be leaving that. All our friends we're leaving...I think it's a bit like nursing somebody through a terminal illness, and even when it happens it's a shock. I think that's how I feel now - bit by bit you're trying to come to terms with the fact that your life's going to change completely. It is like a bereavement.

For Mrs Br. the impact of her husband's redundancy was mediated by her feelings about the community and her own sense of 'belonging' within it. The stress of the move was not only occasioned by his job loss but by her perception of the village's disintegration, and by the impending loss of her own source of social support and meaningful identity outside the home. Indeed, this loss was in fact the loss of an extended family network embedded within the local community. The traditional gender division of labour accepted by Mrs Br. within its historical locally-rooted context was a major factor underlying her present stress: contemplating a future life which would remove this locally-embedded identity and replace it with the bare bones of nuclear family life in a strange environment, meant embracing an identity that was significantly curtailed in terms of social support and autonomy. At the time of interview, this was still a future proposition, but speculation that conflict over gender relations might appear in this relationship under the different social and material conditions on the horizon, is perhaps not unfounded.


**Male re-employment: life after the pit**

Mrs Br. was in a sense poised between two phases in her partner's employment status: that of unemployment, and a new job in a different occupation. The shift was going to involve particular losses for her established identity since it involved moving away from her community role. However, the question of women's responses to spouse re-employment when this spatial disruption is absent, remains. In the previous two sections, we have concentrated on women whose partners were unemployed, but we also included in the interview sample women whose partners had found alternative employment. On the whole, there was less indication of stress and tension here. These men were almost all described by their partners as happier in this new job than they had been at the pit. Even where, as in the vast majority of cases, the replacement work found by the men was significantly inferior to pit work in terms of pay and conditions, all but one of the six women whose husbands were re-employed described them as more content than they had been. Mrs K., for example, had a partner who, having taken redundancy at the time of pit closure, was now a self-employed kitchen fitter. She said that,

> he loves it. I think to do something that he really, really enjoys, it becomes a pleasure as well as earning money. I think he likes it a lot better than going up and down the pit everyday. And I'm glad he's out of the pit.

Her optimism about this was undaunted by the fact that 'he hasn't got a lot on at the moment. At the moment there's a bit of a lull, but we've got our fingrs crossed'. Mrs S., whose husband was now working as a labourer, also felt that her husband was happier now:

> He's out in the open now. He's always wanted to work outside, especially in the Summer, when he can be out in the sun and not down there. He wasn't a faceworker but he did work down the pit, so it's just that he can work outdoors now. I think we're happier now. He is, and that means I am. I'm not worrying that he's down the pit. I know accidents can happen anywhere, but I did used to worry about him. At the latter stage when they worked at the pit, the management weren't bothered about safety. They knew that they'd won, and they'd just sort of got a hold over them. You could ask anybody that.

There was certainly little evidence of ex-miners romanticising the harsh realities of the mines, particularly in the years of demoralisation and closure following the 1984/85 strike. Men who had found alternative employment could more easily put the years of mine-work behind them.

In the cases of re-employment, several factors coincided to reduce stress for women. Firstly, the men were generally happier. Secondly, the partner's attainment of a new job had usually been preceded by a period of unemployment, the memories of which were still fresh in the women's minds: 'At least', said Mrs P., 'it's better than he had been, being on the dole'. Thirdly, the kinds of disruption to household life occasioned by prolonged unemployment (including disruption to gender relations) were largely absent. Things could go on, more or less as before. Re-employment allowed the routines and established gender roles of family life to continue as they had done before redundancy. Even though the men were invariably employed in lower-paid and less secure work, nevertheless they could hold on (at least nominally) to the breadwinner identity. Mrs W., working full-time as a chief clerk, said of the year and a half that her husband was unemployed before finding work as an assistant caretaker at the local college:

> It was much easier for me when my husband wasn't working
> because he took on the extra jobs like hoovering. He didn't
> like to dust, though. He's never done things like ironing and
> that sort of thing, but he'd put a load of washing in and take
> it out. He didn't like housework and he wouldn't be content
> being a house husband. He did it because it helped me, and
> he didn't feel justified in doing nothing when I was working.
> He prefers it now that he's going out to work too.

Invariably, however, when the men started work, things reverted back to the 'occasional help' that had been the pattern when they were miners. For Mrs W., this reversion represented a 'normalisation' of daily life after the difficulties of unemployment, and, like many of the women, her expectations of him fell back - to the extent that she now saw his occasional help as an 'added bonus' not really to be expected:

> Even now, if it's a nice day and he's on afters, I'll put a load
> of towels in the washer in the morning and he'll take them
> out and hang them up before he goes off to work. He's quite
> good really.

Mrs S., who also worked full-time, on school meals, reported that her husband (the re-employed labourer) would now help out with the cooking, but wouldn't do much else:

> He does a lot of cooking. He cooks more than I do in the
> house. Obviously, now, since he's been working he doesn't
> do as much as he used to when he was off. But at the

weekend he'll cook. He used to help me with the cleaning too, but he doesn't do as much now. If he was off work he'd do it. I don't think he can do more than he does now, not now that he's working.

In these accounts, the expected and 'normal' arrangement is for partners to help out regularly only when they are not working. Although both of these women had full-time and demanding jobs, these did not function in the same way as the men's: while their partners' jobs were seen as incompatible with daily domestic labour, there was no such clear dividing line between their own jobs and housework. Mrs W. shopped in her lunch hour and Mrs S. did her 'chores' when she got in from work.

In this way, their partners' re-employment was seen by the women as more demanding than their own paid work, in that it embodied the extra dimension of disqualifying the men from domestic labour. This was the case even though the women routinely defined it as easier than pit-work. Mrs P., for example, described her husband's new job, as a self-employed key-cutter, as

a doddle compared to what he was doing before. When he was working at the pit it was a hard slog - so now, though it's still long hours, it's easier. He used to come home absolutely exhausted. Now, it's long days but he's not tired when he comes in.

In spite of this improvement, there was no corresponding increase in the domestic work he would do compared to when he was at the pit, and, like the other men, his contribution had dramatically reduced since his period of unemployment had ended. This is an effect of the way in which men's work signifies as more than just a job: it occupies a higher position in the wider hierarchy of cultural value. Even where, as in the majority of cases, these new jobs are low-paid service sector ones - like the women's - they still seem capable of claiming the household's central 'breadwinner' status.

In terms of their own psychological well-being women with re-employed partners tended to see the current situation as a continuation rather than a disruption of their daily lives before the pit closed. The sort of tensions over domestic autonomy and the division of labour experienced by the other women did not arise. Instead, the largely traditional domestic organisation of labour simply re-asserted itself as things 'got back to normal'. However, even in the case of male re-employment, women's psychological well-being cannot simply be read off from their partner's employment situation. Mrs C. had not been in paid work while the children were small, but, when it became clear that the pit was to close, she decided to get a job because 'with not knowing what was going to happen, I thought we at least would have one lot of money coming in'. So she found a part-time job at a shop in town. She described the pleasure of having some earning power of her own: 'I thought, I'd got my own money. I could do what I want, and it made a big difference'. Slowly, however, the job began to change. Increasingly, she was given more and more responsibility, and the hours became more like a full time job - often requiring her to do a 3-8 p.m. late shift. At the same time, her 7 year old son began to have problems at school, mainly with truancy. Her husband began to view her job more negatively, especially since, after a very stressful six-month period of unemployment, he had found work himself. Then, unexpectedly, she was sacked over a trivial dispute with her boss about wages. She said, 'I came home and cried my eyes out'. She was given £170 in back pay when she left. Her husband suggested she cheer herself up by buying something in town, but 'I didn't tell him how much I'd actually got. I went to town and spent the lot'.

Mrs C. was now back full-time in the home, and her feelings about this were integral to the stress she felt in her relationship with her husband. This stress crystallised around the issues of her paid work and her childcare and housework. Women may feel ambivalence and guilt about their dual roles as workers and mothers/carers. In Mrs C's case, she was now re-evaluating her identity in the light of the loss of her job. She said that previously, 'it was like being a different person going to work because you weren't just wrapped around the kids'. Now, since she had stopped working outside the home she felt like a 'prisoner'. However, she went on to say that the problems she had been having with her kids were 'all because I was working'. She now felt that her job status had been incompatible with her role as a mother, and that the children had suffered as a consequence. Needless to say, her husband's full-time welding job was not subject to the same contradictions. Since the primary responsibility for bringing up the children remained with her, it was her, and not his, job status that became the site of struggle in the relationship. She explained it like this:

> He prefers me to be at home. [...] When I was working he didn't mind that I was working but there was odd days when he'd say 'you know, the kids aren't the same since you started work - they're still a bit young you know'. I used to think he was just saying that, but now I know he was right. [...] I used

to think 'why should it always be the mums that are with the
kids', but now I think they do need their mum.

In this way, Mrs C. had reconciled herself to the fact of not doing paid work
by reference to legitimated patriarchal values of 'a woman's place' being in
the home. Relinquishing her work identity and conceding the breadwinning
role to her husband was the only coping mechanism available to her, given
the strong cultural expectations attached to women's roles, and the lack of
affordable childcare. While her husband was unemployed, her own earning
capacity was a resource for the family. However, as the hours lengthened
and her husband found work of his own, it became re-coded as a problem.

## Women's job loss: issues of independence and social support

Having considered some of the ways in which domestic strain over male
employment status is experienced by women through particular gendered
formations within the household, I now turn to the question of women's
own relation to the same post-industrial labour market that cost their
partners their jobs. The question of whether men and women tend to react
differently to the experience of unemployment is one to which researchers
have paid considerable attention in recent years. One influential argument
has been that a significant factor in the negative psychological
consequences of unemployment derives from the sudden absence of
meaningful activity and identity that accompanies it. Women, therefore,
are to some extent shielded from this through the continued presence of a
positive identity for them in the domestic sphere (Marshall, 1984).
Recently, this argument has been subjected to a number of criticisms.
Firstly, being an unpaid domestic worker and mother may not be, for many
women, a source of positive identity or valued role (Oakley 1974).
Secondly, this explanation neglects the strategic importance of women's
earning power for their own self-esteem (Coyle, 1984; Popay, 1985). The
research drawn upon here lends weight to these criticisms. The interview
data from women in paid employment suggest that employment-related
factors were significant sources of stress for them.

Four of the women in this interview sample had recently lost jobs that
they had needed and enjoyed. When the local pit closed, for example, Mrs
R. had been made redundant from her full-time job at the pit canteen, which
was a job that she had loved. She had three children of school-age, and her
husband was also unemployed and suffering from ill-health. Now she felt
that everything was 'boring'. She described her day like this:

> It's just the same jobs every day, You get up, make the fire, clean up, wash up, get breakfast. It's just all the same. I'm learning to drive and I came in the other day and I just couldn't be bothered to do a thing. I could have done all the ironing, but you get in a rut. When you're working you do it because you know you're going out to work and you've got to do it. The days seem so long. I just wouldn't have left the pit. I couldn't have wished for a better job.

In this case, the availability of an alternative role in the home was not a substitute for the loss of employment. Mrs R.'s stress was partly derived from having to cope with her husband's depression and poor health after redundancy, but to identify this as the primary cause would be mistaken. Instead, at the root of her present depression and stress was the loss of important sources of social support and a meaningful identity at the pit canteen. She described the atmosphere of support and belonging that this job had provided:

> While I worked at the pit my dad died. He had cancer, and it was awful going through that, but all the men at the pit knew him, and they were really good. they helped me through it, and they helped me through [my husband's] heart attack and they were marvellous. Now I don't feel as though I've got anybody. If you've got troubles now, there's no-one to help you through them. [...] Everything happened at once - my dad died, his mum died and then [my husband] had his heart attack - all at once. The men kept me going because they knew you, they know your life, they know your relations. [...] You've still got friends but it's not the same.

A similar sense of loss was experienced by Mrs B., who was discussed earlier in this chapter. She had also worked at the pit - in a part-time job as wages clerk for British Coal. This job had been steadily deteriorating for a number of years. It had begun as a full-time post with considerable responsibility, affording plenty of opportunity to interact with the miners who came in for their wage packets. The job had since become more and more part-time and casualised as the local pits shut and the remaining miners started to get paid by direct bank credit. Now she was employed on a casual basis for just seven hours every fortnight at a more distant pit, and greatly missed the opportunities for friendship that the job had provided. Like Mrs R. above, she now said 'I very rarely go out now. I've got in a rut'.

She linked her social apathy to the disappearance of her job, and expressed this in terms of the symbolic meaning of the clothes she would wear to work:

> Once I get out I'm fine, it's just that I've got lazy. I've been used to getting dressed up. I've not only done paying out wages and making the packets up: if ever any work came, it was always us casuals they'd ask to do it. I've worked at all the pits in the area, and you've got to go dressed up, you've got to go smart. I've been used to that and just lately, it's just awful - I can't be bothered.

Even though her own work was fast disappearing, though, she still looked forward to going:

> I meet people. There's one or two people that I worked with at [the local pit]. I can have a word with them. Some of the men who used to work at [the local pit] work at Bentley so I have a word with them when they come, and I've made some friends there as well. It's nice. I'd worked with them for a long long time. I enjoy it. I'm not going to leave. They're going to have to get rid of me if they want me to leave.

Mrs B. was now having to confront a future without regular work, feeling that she lacked the qualifications and youth to get another job. At the same time, her husband and son were both newly unemployed and had established a routine of frequent outings to the pub or the snooker club together. Mrs B. was excluded from this activity and thus felt tied to the home in a way that she had not experienced before.

Both Mrs B.'s and Mrs R.'s accounts show that women's own opportunities for employment were often dependent on the mining industry, whether directly or indirectly. Many local small-scale factories had been closing down over the last decade as the local economy declined, and opportunities for women to work were now mainly part-time in local retailing outlets, or in casualised agricultural work. At the time of fieldwork, the major local employer for women in one of the communities - a mushroom farm - had just sacked 70 women, in order to employ only casual workers. This initiated a long dispute, which the women subsequently lost. During my unsuccessful attempts to secure an interview with the local manager, he derisorily referred to the sacked women as 'Scargill's wives'. This comment serves to bring home the fact that the miners' attempts to keep pits operating and working conditions reasonable have been mirrored by countless other small-scale efforts by women to resist the parallel tide of rationalisation and restructuring in their own working areas.

## Conclusion

This chapter has presented a picture of the complex web of interacting factors that mediate the experience of pit closure for women. In considering this experience from different angles I have tried to show how the impact of de-industrialisation on women's lives cannot be reduced to the simple fact of pit closure. It is not only the loss of the pit and its culture of close social networks that causes social strain, as presented by the media campaign alluded to at the beginning of this chapter. Rather, women's position within a declining local labour market is potentially problematic even where men find alternative employment. This is because the question of gendered roles and expectations still means that women are finding their own ability to manoeuvre - to find employment and keep it, but also to carry out the caring and domestic work - severely limited. With the continuing and powerful hold that the male breadwinner ethic exerts on the cultural field, it is often difficult for women to assume the family wage-earning role, even where they can find reasonable employment. As we saw in the case of Mrs M., partners who feel embittered and discarded by the loss of their own breadwinner role, are hardly guaranteed to embrace readily the 'rational' adaptation required by the re-structuring of the labour market. Instead, this process can involve considerable domestic strain on relationships, which, as we have seen, is not a purely psychological or interpersonal response, but a culturally-mediated and embedded one. Even where, as in the case of Mrs Br., this interpersonal strain is avoided, the loss of local ties and spheres of influence as families uproot themselves to find work can produce severe anxieties for women who - in following their husbands' search for work - stand to lose their own independent identities.

Where men do find re-employment within the same locality, this still leaves many women with the same difficulties as before pit closure: their own domestic responsibilities continue as before, and the opportunities for finding their own secure paid employment continue to decline. As we saw in the case of Mrs R., pit closure also removes related jobs for women, and their own redundancy involves the loss of important social networks and spheres of activity. As Mrs R. described, getting a job that could offer the same social opportunities would make the 'biggest difference' to her life:

> I'm not a loner. I like people. If they could open that canteen
> up again tomorrow, it would make my life worth living. But
> they're not going to. I wish it had never shut.

This chapter has demonstrated the advantages of using qualitative methods for gleaning a range and complexity of data that is necessary to make sense of women's relation to pit closure. The qualitative approach can give voice to experiences and feelings that tend to be sidelined in areas, such as mining redundancy, that purport to affect only men. The data can show, for example, how the fact of male unemployment impacts on women's lives in ways that are inevitably bound up with culturally-entrenched formations of masculine and feminine identity. The social and psychological impacts of redundancy should not be seen merely as interpersonal or affective matters - emotional strains that women have to manage as they would any other personal or family crisis. Instead, the onset of unemployment in areas where the male breadwinner ethic has structured social life for generations is inevitably a gender issue, capable of introducing tensions into personal relationships that cannot easily be resolved. In this sense, the expectation of 'rational' and 'obvious' transition from male to female wage-earning, or the hypothesis of an inevitable evolution of gender roles in domestic and childcare labour, need to be seen as highly contingent. Where women have access to mainly part-time work, and where affordable childcare provision is absent, it will always be easier for women to take the path of least resistance and continue in traditional feminine roles. As Morris (1992) points out, the very structure of part-time work for women is built around this assumption. Even where women have access to full-time work, as in Mrs M's case, there still remain considerable obstacles to their assuming the breadwinning role. Relationships can readily disintegrate under this kind of strain.

In presenting data from a community perspective rather then from a narrowly household one, I have also tried to show how women's responses to male unemployment are mediated by their own labour market experiences; restructuring affects their jobs too. The possibility of women assuming the breadwinner role and providing a family wage in the current labour-market conditions of Britain's ex-mining communities is rather remote. Instead, what the data from this study show is that women, as well as men, have access to poorly-paid mainly part-time work that is subject to increasing insecurity. This finding is, of course, not new - and merely confirms the previous work on de-industrialised communities that suggests that working-class families living in these areas face an increasingly socially-isolated and unstable future (Binns and Mars, 1984). It is women who will, it seems, be bearing the major burdens in this post-industrial and post-welfare social landscape.


**Notes**

1.  This study, funded by the ESRC and Joseph Rowntree Trust as part of the Management of Personal Welfare Initiative, was carried out by members of the Community Research Unit, Centre for Media, Communication and Communities Research, Sheffield Hallam University. The project was co-directed by David Waddington and Chas Critcher. Four mining communities were chosen for study: two where the pit had already closed, and two where it was still open, so that a cross-community comparative perspective could be employed.


**References**

Allen, J. and Massey, D. (1988), (eds) *The economy in question,* London, Sage, in association with Open University, .

Bagguley, P., Mark Lawson, J., Shapiro, D., Urry, J., Walby, S. and Warde, A. (1990), *Restructuring: place, class and gender,* London, Sage.

Binns, D. and Mars, G. (1984), Family, Community and Unemployment: A Study in Change, *The Sociological Review,* 32 (1) pp. 662-695.

Bostyn, A. and Wight, D. (1987), Inside a community: values associated with money and time, in S. Fineman (ed.) *Unemployment: personal and social consequences,* London, Tavistock, pp. 138-154.

Campbell, B. (1993), *Goliath: Britain's dangerous places,* London, Methuen.

Coyle, A. (1984), *Redundant women,* London,Virago.

Fagin, L. and Little, B. (1984), *The forsaken families,* Harmondsworth, Penguin.

Gallie, D., Gershuny, J. and Vogler, C. (1993), Unemployment, the household and social networks, in D. Gallie, C. Marsh and C. Vogler, (eds) *Social change and the experience of unemployment,* Oxford, Oxford University Press. pp. 231-263.

Jackson, P. and Walsh, S. (1987), Unemployment in the family, in D. Fryer and P. Ullah (eds) *Unemployed people: social and psychological perspectives,* Milton Keynes, Open University Press. pp. 131-148.

Jahoda, M. (1982), *Employment and unemployment: a social-psychological analysis,* Cambridge, Cambridge University Press.

Laite, J. and Halfpenny, P. (1987), Employment, unemployment and the domestic division of labour in Fryer, D. and Ullah, P.(eds) *Unemployed people,* Milton Keynes, Open University Press, pp.162-184.

Marshall, G. (1984), On the significance of women's employment, its neglect and significance, *The Sociological Review,* 32, (2) pp. 234-59

Martin, R. and Wallace, J. (1984), *Working women in recession,* Oxford, Oxford University Press.

Massey, D. (1984), *Spatial divisions of labour,* London, Macmillan

Mattinson, J. (1988), *Work, love and marriage: the impact of unemployment,* London, Duckworth.

McKee, L. and Bell, C. (1985), Marital and family relations in times of male unemployment, in B. Roberts, R. Finnegan and D. Gallie, (eds) *New approaches to economic life,* Manchester, Manchester University Press, pp. 387-399

McKee, L. and Bell, C. (1986), His unemployment, her problem: the domestic and marital consequences of male unemployment', in S. Allen, A. Watson, K. Purcell and S. Wood, (eds) *The experience of unemployment,* London, Macmillan. pp. 134-149.

Morris, L. (1985), Renegotiation of the domestic division of labour in the context of male redundancy in B. Roberts, R. Finnegan and D. Gallie (eds) *New approaches to economic life.* Manchester, Manchester University Press. pp. 400-416.

Morris, L. (1992), Domestic labour and employment status among married couples: a case study in Hartlepool, *Capital and Class*: 49

Oakley, A. (1974), *The sociology of housework,* Martin Robertson, Oxford.

Pahl, R. (1984), *Divisions of labour,* Oxford, Blackwell.

Popay, J. (1985), Women, the family and unemployment in P. Close, and R. Collins, (eds) *Family and economy in modern society,* London, Macmillan, pp.174-191.

Waddington, D., Dicks, B. and Critcher, C. (1992), Community responses to pit closure, *Community Development Journal,* 29 (2) pp. 141-150.

Wheelock, J. (1990), *Husbands at home,* London and New York, Routledge

# 3 From 'honorary chap' to mother: combining work in the professions with motherhood

*Janet Stephens*

## Introduction

Despite equal access to education and training, and equal opportunities legislation being in place for over twenty years, women still stumble on the block of dominant gender ideology in Western society (Rees 1992). This ideology persistently locates women primarily in the domestic sphere; ultimately responsible for the physiological and psychological well-being of their family members. However, there are growing numbers of women who achieve a high level of education and training, and use these achievements to penetrate areas of paid employment previously dominated by men (Spencer and Podmore 1987; Greed 1991). Women who gain entry to a traditionally male dominated profession, such as medicine, take on the status of 'honorary chap' (Elston 1991). This status is best maintained by adopting male career patterns and attitudes towards working, and is necessarily relinquished when women opt out of full-time working in their profession. Analyses of data gathered *inter alia* by the Women and Employment Survey (Martin and Roberts 1984) have all reported the downward occupational mobility women encounter on their return to paid employment after a career break. This is often due to their labour market participation resuming on a part-time basis. Part-time work has become synonymous with less-skilled, lower status work. Most of the studies on part-time work have concentrated on women in low status, low paid jobs (for a review of the research on employment and family life carried out in the UK over the last fifteen years see Brannen *et al* 1994). The reason for this is simply that most part-time work *is* of low status and is therefore low paid. However: increasingly, women working in the professions are unwilling to use the traditional coping strategies of women in top jobs (Breakwell 1985), of adopting 'male' career patterns and values and instead are turning to 'flexible' working (including pursuing part-time routes).

The research discussed in this chapter focuses on the career patterns of a sample of professional women in Wales, specifically women doctors in hospital medicine, who are working part-time in order to combine their careers with motherhood. The aim of the study on which this chapter draws was to unravel the experiences of this group of women in their 'public' and 'private' lives on a day-to-day basis. The data are taken from a qualitative research project on trainee doctors; who are women, mothers and training part-time. The three characteristics are significant. An effect of motherhood is that women often return to work on a part-time basis.

Due to the nature of medical career patterns, working part-time can create particular problems for (women) doctors. Although medical students qualify as doctors after their first degree, 'training' in hospital medicine is not complete until the doctor has worked through the grades of house officer, senior house officer (SHO), registrar and senior registrar (SR). It is usual for doctors to remain at each grade for around three years, reaching consultant status in their late thirties/early forties. Professional examinations have to be taken for the doctor to be accredited by the Royal Colleges, in order to achieve the move from the grade of SHO to registrar, and from registrar to SR. Doctors are also expected to carry out research and publish material throughout their career. The combined factors of grade, professional examinations and publications make up the 'typical' successful career of a doctor in hospital medicine. Successful career progression for doctors is typically to follow this pattern on a full-time basis.

The women doctors in my sample were all participants in the *Flexible Training Scheme for Doctors and Dentists with Family Commitments or Disability*; a part-time training programme designed to meet the specific needs of hospital doctors at distinct points in the life course, on the assumption that they will resume full-time careers as their children grow older. Originally entitled the *Part-time Training Scheme for Women Doctors*, the scheme was set up by the National Health Executive in 1969 as a response to the perceived demographic challenge faced by the Executive as employers. Seeking to retain their investment in highly trained staff, women were encouraged to return to the labour market after a career break for childrearing. The *Flexible Training Scheme* is an acknowledgement that both men and women (although as the original title suggests, it was thought that women would have a greater need for the scheme) had special needs at distinct points in their career. It was intended to facilitate their continued training to consultant status. The National Health Service Executive has a stated commitment that by the year 2000, five percent of all staff will work on a flexible basis - in the region of Wales, the location for this research, the present figure stands at just one percent, the lowest in the United Kingdom.

**Research design and process**

The women doctors interviewed for the project on which this chapter draws all had differing needs related to their family careers, which had propelled them towards flexible training. Some could be identified as women returners who were resuming their careers after several years marking time off the training track. Others were trying to construct an uninterrupted career path in hospital medicine. During the research period the status of several of the doctors in the study changed: some achieved consultant status (3); transferred out of the area (2); withdrew from the training scheme to move to job share posts (2); withdrew to continue to work full-time (1); decided not to return to work after career break (1).

The value of qualitative research methods to study this theme was their potential for uncovering the differences among professional women who are mothers. Through ethnographic interviews it became possible to unravel their views of the reality of their career and family lives (Reinharz 1992). The questionnaire method of research was considered but rejected as not having the scope to represent and give adequate voice to the doctors' experiences. Although attempts have been made to 'overcome the tendency of surveys to compartmentalize or fracture women's experiences' (May 1993 p.89), the interview method is generally used to 'yield rich sources of data on people's experiences, opinions, aspirations and feelings' (May 1993 p.91). In all, twenty-two interviews were carried out for the projects, fourteen with women who were following the *Flexible Training Scheme* in Wales. Another five interviews were with trainee doctors who were on the waiting list for the scheme. Three interviews were also carried out with those who allocate the resources of the scheme and who are in charge of its adminstration: the Chief Medical Officer for Wales; the Postgraduate Dean of Medical Education; and the Convenor of the Flexible Training Course. In this chapter I draw upon the interview data from those women doctors following the Flexible Training Scheme and two of the course administrators.

Interviews with the women doctors had two main phases. The first part of each interview generated information on family and work histories. Semi-structured questions were used for this section so that generalities and comparability of experience among the doctors' histories could be explored. Background information was gathered, such as which speciality the doctor trained in and how many children she had. This part of the interview was also used as a period of ice-breaking (Yeandle 1984). The function of the ice-breaker is to relax both the interviewee and the interviewer, and to set the scene. Those being interviewed need to be convinced that it has relevance to their lives and that they can contribute valuable information to the research project (Reinharz 1992). Demographic information was gathered to build up individual career histories. Parallel to the work history, family formation histories were constructed. The two histories were then superimposed during data analysis to trace how each doctor had moved in and out of the labour market corresponding to family status. Using a semi-structured interview schedule in this way, individual life histories up to the point of data collection could be mapped out (the interviews were tape-recorded and later transcribed in full).

Central to the aims of the research project was the exploration of the meanings and interpretations of the doctor's own life history. The second part of the interviews were more ethnographic in nature, issues and themes which the women had identified as important to their family/work biographies were focussed upon. The women were encouraged to talk about these in more detail, offering explanation and interpretation as they went along. This was a voyage of self-discovery for some as they had perhaps not had the opportunity to articulate feelings to an interested outsider before (Finch 1984). One interview was with a Senior House Officer who was waiting to hear whether her funding had been approved for the flexible training scheme:

> No, its alright, I am tired but its quite therapeutic isn't it, I
> mean it is depressing but its better for me to think about it ...
> at least you are interested in what happens.
>
> (Senior House Officer, Psychiatry, two children)

Another doctor used the interview to rehearse her dilemma of whether or not to return to work at all following her career break; she saw only limited options available to her. She talked through what she saw as the pros and cons of different types of career and childcare possibilities. Off tape, at the end of the interview she expressed concern as to whether or not I had gathered relevant information for my research. During this interview I had put away my questions and listened to her talk about what was obviously of utmost concern to her. I prompted her in her reflections to aid the flow of talk (May 1993). Her articulation of the practicalities of what course her life should take later helped me to focus on decision-making processes within family units and allocation of household resources (see section below).

During the interviews, I not only asked questions but also answered questions (Oakley 1981). At the outset of the interview the nature of the research project was explained and my own identity as a researcher and a mother were established. When discussing childcare I was often asked what type of childcare I used. This was then measured against their experiences in terms of cost of childcare, available hours or qualifications of staff, and comparisons were made. One senior registrar reflected on the childcare she used:

> ... yes, that has made me see really how good she's been actually, she does have her problems at the moment ... yet despite that she's not really skived or turned up late, yes you're making me think how good she's been.
>
> (Senior Registrar, Anaesthetics, two children)

The value of indepth, qualitative interviewing is that confusions and contradictions can be drawn out in a reflective manner by the interviewee. This methodology yielded rich, descriptive data about a sample of professional women at distinct points in their life-course. The following sections of this chapter highlight themes which emerged from the interview data: the first section examines how family status affects career decisions and so impacts on women doctors' career patterns. I then go on to explore the status of working part-time in hospital medicine, the tensions between home and the labour market, and decisions about child care.

## Gendered career patterns

Within the National Health Service there has always been provision for doctors to *work* (rather than *train*) part-time, an option mostly taken up by women and overseas doctors (Dowie 1987). In medicine the move off the training track is generally viewed as professional suicide. The result is career stagnation, as one senior registrar explained:

> Yes, well its very difficult in medicine because the only other alternative would be to work at what they call clinical assistant sessions ... there's no promotion and no training involved, you could do them for ten years and at the end of it you are no better off than at the beginning.
>
> (Senior Registrar, Genetics, 4 children)

Uprooting and moving to different geographical locations is part and parcel of career progression within hospital medicine. This had impacted on the women doctors' decisions about work pattern options. Across occupations, women generally tend to follow the geographic mobility demands of their husband's career. This can have an extremely disruptive effect on the following partner's career, as a woman doctor who was on senior registrar grade explained:

> ... and every time we moved it meant that whatever I'd arranged for myself it went by the board and I had to start all over again which usually meant that you had to change specialties.
>
> (Senior Registrar, Genetics, four children)

Except in two instances, the doctors interviewed were married to other doctors, and, in all instances of these same-profession marriages, the male partner was on a higher grading than the female partner. However, in response to questions of why the husband was on a higher grading than themselves, the answers given did not include older age of male partner (1 exception), or more success at professional examinations. On pregnancy, the women had taken a career break and so their career had fallen behind their husband's. When asked to compare their own career pattern with their husband's, the male partner's career came first as a rational response to the fact that women bear children and so *necessarily* take at least some time out of the labour market. The consequences of family formation devolved solely onto the mother:

> Well, its difficult you see, one of us had to do it and it was him ... his career went very smoothly, he did it by the book and did all the right things.
>
> (Senior Registrar, Genetics, four children)

During the interviews the suggestion that the male partners career was advantaged exactly for the reason that the woman had taken time out for childrearing was met with some hostility. Long term planning was defined in terms of joint decision-making as one registrar made explicit to me:

> Yes, we made a joint decision to do that, I didn't fall in with his plans, we had *our* plans of what they would be.
>
> (Registrar, Public Health, two children)

The ability to rationalise a disadvantaged career can be interpreted as a coping mechanism. Brannen and Moss (1991) note that their 'managing mothers' (1994) tended to make excuses for their male partners on the grounds of other, mainly breadwinning responsibilities, praising them for the activities they did do. They argue that women adopt a rational view as a strategy to avoid domestic conflict and also to avoid having to recognise inequality in their relationships. While acknowledging that their partner's career had advanced at the expense of their own, personal maternal needs were cited by some of the women doctors as the reason for time off the training track:

> Well, thats how it came about but that was how it was going to come about ... I got very broody so we made a decision and I always wanted to stay at home with mine for a bit, I mean thats just the way I am, so we said, well you carry on and then when I decide and if I decide, then we'll take it from there.
>
> (Senior Registrar, Paediatrics, three children)

For those women who have marked time and now wish to return to work 'properly' or feel they need to combine working with motherhood, flexible training can be the ideal option. However, there are many drawbacks to working part-time in a profession traditionally dominated by male career patterns and values. The next part of this chapter looks at the reality of part-time work in a somewhat hostile environment.

### Being (m)other at work: the stigma of working part-time

Being a professional in hospital medicine is still rigidly viewed as a job that necessitates 24 hour availability, with anything less seen as a 'casual' commitment. The Chief Medical Officer for Wales was interviewed as *she* is a significant gatekeeper of resources allocated to funding postgraduate medical education. I asked for her views on how the *Flexible Training Scheme* should benefit women working in Wales. She argued that until the adherence to 'macho' style working patterns changes within hospital medicine, part-time trainees will face difficulties with their consultants and colleagues. There are very few funded places for doctors training on a flexible basis in Wales (fourteen at time of data collection). Often these doctors are historically the first, and usually the only part-timer in their department, their specialty, or even within the whole hospital. This can lead to problems as colleagues and superiors have little understanding of what 'flexible' training means, as the following extract highlights:

> I'm the first person to do obs and gyny part-time so I'm breaking new ground, so people don't really understand what being part-time means.
>
> (Registrar, Obstetrics and Gynaecology, 2 children)

The goodwill of consultants and colleagues is extremely valuable in promoting junior careers. Assumptions of low career attachment were expressed overtly to Dr. Northwood when she made public her decision to seek part-time training:

> They just stop taking you seriously in the department ... I have been told in front of other consultants at my review that did I not think that commitments now lay elsewhere rather than with my career.
>
> (Senior Registrar, Oncology, 1 child, pregnant)

Many of the women reported that colleagues assumed they had a low attachment to working, which can have devastating consequences for career progression. Prejudice from colleagues and consultants was not always expressed openly but was experienced as a more subtle attitude, difficult to pin down but nevertheless there;

> ... often it's more a way they say things than the things they do say, you know a rather dismissive attitude ... people couldn't believe that I was actually being paid to work these hours .. as if my work was hardly worth paying for, implied not actually spoken.
>
> (Senior Registrar, Histopathology, one child)

Another experience of the part-time doctor is exclusion from the collegiality that those on a full-time programme enjoy. A senior house officer argued that in order to get through as much work as possible in the limited time available to her she often worked through her lunch hour and took no breaks. The result was that she was self-excluded from discussions, or the social networking that took place in a general way during the day:

> I think if you work part-time in medicine you stand out a bit because you're not one of the chaps ... that sort of sense of cameraderie is excluded for part-timers.
>
> (Senior House Officer, Psychiatry, one child)

Trying to retain credibility as still being one of the chaps, despite diverging from the temporal norm of full-time engagement, is extremely difficult in hospital medicine. All the doctors interviewed reported negative effects at work which they saw as being connected to their part-time status.

Employment status also impacted on the private dimension of the doctors' lives. Mothering is regarded as a 24 hour commitment with poor provision for part-time participation. In contrast to men, women's role sets are additive in nature rather than being sequential. When women leave home for the workplace they do not stop being a mother, and matters related to the domestic sphere intrude on their professional lives, particularly at crisis points such as times of illness. The next section examines how the women resolved the issue of replicating their presence at home.

**Substituting the mother**

Mothering is often understood to be the exclusive domain of women, best carried out by the biological mother (Brannen *et al* 1994). Substitute mothering is almost always undertaken by other women. The social construction of the role of mother means that the responsibility for the well-being and harmony of those living in her domestic sphere ultimately lies with the mother (Phoenix 1991). Mothers who work are under pressure to provide better than 'good enough' mothering. By following a professional career path, they are challenging prevailing attitudes which dictate what women should do, when and how. The British Social Attitudes Survey (1988) found that 93 percent of respondents believed that the best scenario for families with children under 5 years was the male partner in full-time employment with the female partner remaining at home to care for the children. However, both women and men agreed that women could engage in part-time work without their families being adversely affected, and successive surveys report that the option of men in full-time work and women in part-time work has become increasingly more socially acceptable (Brannen *et al* 1994).

During the interviews, it emerged that negative effects of part-time working were consciously weighed against the perceived positive gains made in the domestic sphere. The most important gain women talked about was the extra time they gained to spend with their children. I have explored the issues of time, timing and temporality as they relate to this research in detail elsewhere (Stephens 1996). Time management is inextricably linked to the day-to-day experiences of mothers working in the professions. The doctors saw it as important to spend all time outside that allocated to paid work in active participation with their children's lives, particularly when the children were of pre-school age. Some defined time with their children as needing to be 'quality' time and were resentful of having to do housework when their time at home was so limited:

> I'm not going to spend my time on the weekend that I have actually got with the children doing cleaning, I'm not

prepared to do that ... because the time that I have is very precious.

(Senior Registrar, Psychiatry, three children)

One doctor perceived time as a finite amount: that time spent doing the housework subtracted from the time she could spend with her daughter. She rejected the possibility of having available to her the necessary time to do both and decided she would need to buy in domestic labour when she returned to work:

> I wouldn't want to come home to clean so that when I had time with Lianne I wouldn't be running round doing the washing and cleaning, I would actually spend some time with her ... I don't want to do the washing up but I do want to look after Lianne.
>
> (Senior House Officer, Psychiatry, eight month baby)

Even though the doctors interviewed tended to view housework negatively as wasted time, not all engaged paid domestic labour. This was not always due to lack of financial resources. More often they described feelings of guilt at hiring others to do 'their' work, as they understood the management of the domestic sphere to be their individual responsibility. Because they were doing part-time work they were physically located in the home for more hours than their partners. The outcome (that they did the housework) was therefore perceived as a rational response, as was the tendency to explain the partner's overall lack of participation in the domestic sphere. Wheelock (1990) argues that with women's increasing participation in the labour market and their increased economic independence, the domestic division of labour will become less rigidly defined, although she acknowledges that is to some extent dependent on the employment status of both partners. Other research has highlighted the fact that the traditional division of labour operates across class (Gregson and Lowe 1993) and regardless of employment status (Morris 1995). The interview data from this research highlight how responsibility for the domestic sphere tends to be divided along traditional lines as a 'natural' and rational response to differing engagement in the workplace. Employment status is a factor which impacts on how the home is managed. Although women are present in the public sphere they take on sole responsibility for the private sphere. This is reflected in how incomes are allocated within dual earner families. Research on the allocation of resources within families shows that while women pay for childcare, men pay for mortgages (Marsh and Arber 1992) and this was also found to be a tendency among the women doctors interviewed.

> I mean I do 40 hours a week almost, but you only get paid for three days which is okay because I've got a partner who earns enough money to support us, but my wage only just covers the childcare and nursery fees and things like that.
>
> (Senior Registrar, Obstetrics and Gynaecology, two children)

This extract illustrates how dual earner families divide responsibility for payment of goods and services. The implications of such differential allocations of earnings are that unequal value is placed on men's and women's earnings. The male partner's wage can be seen as a non-varying essential as it pays for the absolute necessities of shelter and warmth. The woman's wage is in danger of being defined as not 'essential' because a large proportion of it is spent on covering her absence from home. The practice of women using their wage to cover childcare costs is explained as a rational response by women rather than being understood as placing them at a disadvantage in their domestic relationships.

**Childcare options**

As childcare is seen as a replacement for the mother and not both parents, the task of choosing the appropriate substitute to match the needs of her children is taken on by her. Leaving aside for now the point highlighted by this and other research (Brannen and Moss 1991) that it is the mother who needs to know that the children are safe for her to have the 'peace of mind' to work (suggesting that men are not expected to have such concerns); this does mean that she is the parent who picks up and drops off the children; she has the physical task of paying wages, and so has more face to face contact with the employee. As long as the implicit understanding between partners is that women pay for substitute mother-care, rather than partners paying for childcare enabling them both to engage in paid employment, then women will face the economic dilemma of whether it is 'worth' her going to work, only to pay someone else to do 'her job'.

> Well all my wages have always gone on the children so that I can go to work ... I go to work for my sanity not for the money.
>
> (Senior Registrar, Genetics, four children)

Bought-in childcare is used to cover the mother's absence from the home while she was at work. Professional women often have no local kin support networks which is the preferred type of childcare used for mothers who work (Brannen 1991). A consequence of a professional career is geographical mobility - often away from family and kin. Women are left to manage childcare individualistically with no clear idea of local resources, pay scales and working conditions of those offering childcare services. This can be a daunting task as many of the women in this study reported. Some used local nanny agencies initially but argued that information transmitted by word-of- mouth from other mothers was more valuable in finding someone with the qualifications they wanted. When asked to state the criteria used when hiring childcare, these women ranked certificated qualifications lower than flexibility, reliability and honesty;

> I was looking for someone with training in childcare but my friend asked if I wanted to nanny share with her and that has been ideal. I can trust her with the children and she is really flexible which is what I needed.
>
> (Senior Registrar, Radiology, two children)

Social Services Departments maintain a list of local registered childminders at their Family Centres. This service will in future be put on-line for general use for example in public libraries but as yet is not available. Most of the doctors found out about childminders from other mothers at schools or playgroups, and not from social service lists;

> My childcare took a bit longer to set up because I was asking the other mums if they could recommend someone and they told me that a place had become free with a local mum.
>
> (Registrar, Paediatrics, one child)

Flexibility is ranked high on the list of necessary criteria as hospital doctors often have to work late at short notice. Flexibility was defined as being able to keep the child/ren longer than the agreed hours, or to change arranged care days if necessary. In the absence of truly flexible childcare and informal childcare networks, doctors use their partners as 'emergency' cover. This is often to bolster their own credibility at work which they see as being destroyed by the absolute need to pick up children punctually. One registrar working in paediatrics needed her husband to cover her absence at home to counter what she perceived as negative reactions of her colleagues to her work timetable:

> So I say to him [partner], look this is the one day that I need
> to have time when I'm not rushing off because if you say
> 'well I've got to go at five' they look at you and say oh well,
> you're casual, you don't really mean what you're doing.
>
> (Registrar, Paediatrics, one child)

When children enter full-time education, school becomes the main form of childcare. However, school holidays are still a problem. Parents often take separate annual leave to cover the long vacation period which means that time spent together as a family unit is reduced.

> We did have some time together but I either took days off
> and used up all my holiday, or my husband took a day off or
> my mother-in-law managed to come down and have a few
> days with the children.
>
> (Senior Registrar, Genetics, four children)

The school holidays are often the time when extended family members combine a visit with childcare. During term time some of the children attended the after-school club or waited in the library before school started in the morning. Childcare to cover *inset* (teacher training) days where the school is closed to pupils has to be organised at quite short notice:

> When you least want them they throw in *inset* days just to
> totally confuse the timetable that has taken you ages to get
> together, then you have these dreaded one off days that you
> just cannot prepare for.
>
> (Registrar, Public Health, two children)

What emerged from the interviews was that childcare concerns do not end or even particularly ease when the child enters full-time education. One doctor stressed that needs were different but just as time-consuming and demanding for the mother who is principally engaged in organising their activities:

> No it doesn't really get easier its just that their needs change,
> so you spend most of your time as a ferrying service going to
> beavers [sic] and swimming and then rugby practice or choir,
> its always something and you have to remember what day
> everything is on and make sure kit is clean or whatever.
>
> (Senior Registrar, Psychiatry, three children)

Most of the women stated explicitly that, quite apart from career progression, the motivation for training part-time was because they wanted to participate in their children's lives which included being the one to take them to and from school when possible and acting as their 'ferrying service'. They saw such participation as part of being a mum, which children also value:

> I've made a point of picking Caragh up from nursery as often as I can ... I mean [nanny] could do it, she's here and is paid for that but I think its important for them as well that you show an interest and Caragh really loves it if I pick her up ... its only a little thing but its important to her.
>
> (Senior Registrar, Radiology, two children)

Because of the identification of distinct qualities linked to activities which made up the role of 'mum' I was interested to see whether they saw a time when they would give these up. When asked whether they expected to resume their careers on a full-time basis most replied that they would prefer to remain in part-time participation. Even though the consequences for career progression were viewed in extreme negative terms, the benefits of having 'extra' time with their children were seen as too great to relinquish. This conflicts with how those who organise the *Flexible Training Scheme* expect women's career patterns to proceed. Availability of places operate on a drop off-come on basis, and the scheme is designed to be used as a problem solving mechanism at distinct points of (women's) life course. The convenor of the course explained her concerns about the *Flexible Training Scheme* not being flexible enough:

> ...the scheme has been set up with every good intention but it doesn't actually serve the function that it is supposed to serve, it is not flexible enough.

The only way to resolve this would mean a massive expansion of flexible training, especially in Wales where the current percentage participation is one percent of overall 'man'power. It would mean that the provision of part-time training would change to being needs-led instead of funding-led. For this ideal type of scenario to occur the whole concept of being a professional in hospital medicine would have to radically alter.

**Conclusions**

For the majority of women, the preferred time of childbearing and rearing coincides with that period of intensive training in the professions. One option for professional women to avoid career stagnation is to follow a programme of flexible training at points of need in their life course. However, the main conclusions drawn from the data discussed in this chapter are that attitudinal barriers are as difficult to overcome for hospital doctors as in other professions or occupations (Collinson *et al* 1990), despite enabling policies such as the *Flexible Training Scheme*. It became clear during the interviews that women had difficulty overcoming barriers they couldn't 'pin down' or name. Colleagues and consultants had certain perceptions of part-time working which impacted negatively upon the doctors' careers. The women strongly believed that colleagues perceived part-time trainees' commitment to working as less than their own. This was sometimes openly articulated, but more often it was implied through a dismissive attitude. The very fact they were mothers positioned them as 'other', which negatively affected their legitimate claim to professional status. For women returners, the *Flexible Training Scheme* is the only way back onto the training track. One doctor acknowledged that without the option of part-time training she would not have resumed her career:

> Yes, it was so difficult coming back. If it wasn't for part-time training I wouldn't be in medicine now, there's no doubt in my mind.
> > (Registrar, Community Health, four children)

The negative effects of part-time working were weighed against perceived benefits of having more time with their children. Part-time training was seen as the best available option and many stressed that they were happy with their current mix of work and family life.

> I feel very smug, I feel as though I've got the best of both worlds.
> > (Registrar, Public Health, two children)

The doctors felt they had gained valuable 'extra' time to be with their children and to participate in activities which they saw as integral to 'being a mum'. Such activities did not lessen as their children grew older and overall part-time training was seen as an enabling policy for women to combine their work with their family lives. Once they were established on a flexible training programme, the doctors expressed a reluctance to imagine a time when they would return to full-time work. Their reflections on their work and family lives showed a tendency to view part-time training as the best of the available options.

Through qualitative interviews such reflections were articulated. The value of qualitative research methods lies in the opportunity for building a rapport between interviewer and interviewee, thus allowing tentative or submerged meanings to surface. Focusing on key themes and issues and encouraging the women to expand on these, meant that they had a chance to reflect during the interview on how their career might proceed, which options were available to them, or generally just to 'let off steam' about the problems and difficulties they had to overcome. These ranged from perceived attitudinal problems at work to the practicalities of arranging day-to-day childcare provision. The method of building up career and family history patterns through interviews highlights gendered career patterns for professional women, specifically women doctors in hospital medicine. Employment status was shown to impact on home management. Coping mechanisms adopted by professional women in issues of childcare and household management confirm that, across class, the traditional pattern of women bearing primary responsibilty for the domestic sphere still applies.

**Note**

I would like to thank Jane Pilcher and Amanda Coffey for their comments on earlier drafts of this chapter.

**References**

Brannen, J., Meszaros, G., Moss, P. and Poland, G. (1994), *Employment and family life: a review of the research in the UK (1980-1994)*, London, University of London, (Thomas Coram Research Unit).

Brannen, J. and Moss, P. (1991), *Managing mothers: dual earner households after maternity leave*, London, Macmillan.

Breakwell, G. (1985), *The quiet rebel : women at work in a man's world*, London, Century.

Collinson, D.L., Knights, D. and Collinson, M. (1990), *Managing to discriminate*, London, Routledge

Dowie, R. (1987), *Postgraduate medical education and training: the system in England and Wales*, London, King Edward's Hospital Fund for London.

Elston, M. (1991), The politics of professional power: medicine in a changing health service, in Gabe, J., Calnan, M. and Bury, M. (eds) *The sociology of the health service,* London, Routledge, pp.58-88.

Greed, C. (1991), *Surveying sisters: women in a traditional male profession,* London, Routledge.

Gregson, N. and Lowe, M. (1993), Renegotiating the domestic division of labour? A study of dual career households in north east and south east England, *The Sociological Review,* 41(3), pp.475-504.

Martin, J. and Roberts, C. (1984), *Women and employment: a lifetime perspective,* London, HMSO.

Marsh, C. and Arber, S. (eds) (1992), *Families and households: divisions and change,* London, Macmillan.

May, T. (1993), *Social research: issues, methods and process,* Buckingham, Open University Press.

Morris, L. (1995), *Social divisions: economic decline and social structural change,* London, UCL Press Limited.

Oakley, A. (1981), Interviewing women: a contradiction in terms in Roberts, H. (ed.) *Doing feminist research,* London, Routledge and Kegan Paul. pp.30-61.

Phoenix, A., Woollett, A. and Lloyd, E. (eds) (1991), *Motherhood: meanings, practices and ideologies,* London, Sage.

Rees, T. (1992), *Women and the labour market,* London, Routledge.

Reinharz, S. (1992), *Feminist methods in social research,* Oxford, Oxford University Press.

Spencer, A. and Podmore, D. (eds) (1987), *In a man's world: essays on women in male-dominated professions,* London, Tavistock.

Stephens, J. (1996), A fight for her time: challenges facing professional mothers in *Women's Studies International Forum* Special Issue, Vol. 20, June 1996 proceedings from conference Gender Perspectives on Household Issues, 8-9th April 1995, Reading.

Wheelock, J. (1990), *Husbands at home: the domestic economy in a post industrial society.* London, Routledge.

Yeandle, S. (1984), *Women's working lives: patterns and strategies,* New York, Tavistock

# 4 Childish things: Men, ageing and violence

*Julie Owen*

....this was all like, ten, fifteen years ago now....

(Simon).

## Introduction

This chapter will focus on the experiences of male victims of violence. It will argue that the experiencing of violence, and strategies for coping with these experiences are significantly gendered. For many men violence, and anxieties around personal safety, are 'safely' negotiated through age. The statuses associated with maleness, and in particular ageing maleness, allow many men to successfully limit or bound experiences of victimization, and fears of a reoccurrence of this victimization. This is in sharp contrast to the experiences of violence and anxieties around personal safety that many women face. Women's experiences as victims of violence are not in conflict with their social identity as women. For both men and women, violence and victimization are linked to their doing of gender, but in very different ways. I argue in this chapter that being a man, or rather being a man of a particular and transient age range, allows many men the opportunity of using both choice and control over their experiences as male victims of violence.

*Usage and abusage: the language of victimization*

The uses of particular words to describe and illuminate the issues of victimization must be reflective and open. As in any piece of social research, the researcher must be aware, and make the reader aware, of the ways in which certain terms are used. In this chapter, a number of central descriptors are used; in particular: violence, victim, masculinities, choice, and control. A brief explanation of how I use these terms is given below.

Violence is used, purposefully, to cover a range of behaviours which hurt, intimidate, or degrade the person they are aimed at. This is not meant to obscure the differences between forms of violence, which are very real and varied. What it sets out to do is to link behaviours which I believe have their root cause (and primary impact) in structural inequalities of power (Kelly, 1989). Likewise, victim and victimization are contentious words. Neither word is meant to imply a static or powerless state. The word victim is necessary to locate agency for the violent act/s with the aggressor and the term victimization is essential in highlighting the experience of violence as a dynamic and shifting process.

My conscious use of the word *masculinities* is part of an attempt to problematize the constructions of gender, recognising the varying and sometimes conflicting identities which constitute being a man. This endeavour, and indeed this chapter, owes much to the continuing debates within the developing literatures on men and masculinities (see Connell 1995). Whilst I recognise the multi-layered nature of masculine identifications, I still recognise gender as the primary defining factor in experiencing violence for most women and men. This is not to minimise differences; for example of gay men and lesbian women, men and women of colour, whose experiences of violence may be significantly affected by these other identities.

The issues of choice and control are very important when focusing on the experiences of victims of violence. The central element to most experiences of violence is a shattering loss of control. Much of the literature on strategies for dealing with victimization is concerned with the ways in which this sense of control (over one's body, one's environment) may be regained. Essential to this project of control is the issue of choice. Choice in how to act (as a potential victim; as a victim; as a survivor); choice in how to define the situation; in how to respond to the violent act/s; in who (if any) to involve. This chapter will argue that men, as victims of violence (as in many other areas of social life), have more opportunities to engage in choice and demonstrate control than do female victims of violence.

### Qualitative methods, feminist methodology and male research participants

This chapter is based on the process and findings of a project exploring the relationships between gender and violence. The project was rooted firmly in feminist theory and heavily influenced by interpretivist traditions in social research. Thirty semi-structured in-depth interviews were carried out with seventeen men and thirteen women between the ages of twenty one and thirty nine. The interviews focused on experiences of violence, as victims. The active strategies employed by women and men in order to deal with these experiences were explored. The interviews were also concerned with the everyday negotiations of personal safety that women and men may (or may not) engage in.

The methods described in this chapter are qualitative. Whilst the influences of theoretical preferences are strong, the primary factors determining choice of method in this project were ultimately the demands of the topic and the research question itself. In this case the demands of such a sensitive and complex topic seemed to call for qualitative methods. A focus on the dynamics surrounding violent event/s and the processes of becoming a victim necessitated the use of methods which enabled a flexible approach to data collection exploring the creation of meaning and the active experiencing of a variety of situations. Qualitative methods allow the researcher to explore the everyday world of the research participants, to produce research grounded in their experiences (Jones, 1985; Reinhartz, 1992). This research aimed to collect in-depth data through which the research participants could speak in their own words. Quantitative research methods have been criticised for their inability to capture the meaning of everyday human activity (Hammersley & Atkinson 1983). They are also in danger of eliciting only superficial or stereotypical responses from participants. This is not to deny that much valuable work has been done in this area using quantitative methods; establishing the extent of the problem of violence against women, for example. Quantitative methods may be both revealing and (if sensitively applied) potentially less traumatic than qualitative methods in exploring areas such as child abuse. This suggestion also highlights that the often taken for granted orthodoxy, that feminist research is primarily qualitative research need not necessarily be the case.

Interpretivist and feminist critiques of traditional, quantitative social research, are primarily located around epistemological, rather than necessarily methodological, assumptions. They criticise positivist claims that science is objective or neutral (Morgan, 1990; Ramazanoglu, 1992) and claim, in contrast, that rigorous scholarship is that which acknowledges the socially situated nature of the process, producer and product of research (Hammersley & Atkinson, 1983; Laws, 1990; Morgan, 1990; Stanley, 1991; Stanley & Wise, 1991; Aldridge, 1993; Reinhartz, 1992).

Having acknowledged the social position of the researcher as both woman and feminist, the question remains why the project is so involved in the experiences and identities of men. Partly this is in recognition of the fact that '[w]omen do not inhabit a single-sexed universe' (Stanley & Wise 1991, p.44). Little research has focused on the experiences of men as victims (notable exceptions include Stanko, 1990; Stanko & Hobdell, 1993; Herek & Berrill, 1992). Primarily it is a result of the proposal that there is something revealing in the relationships between masculinity and violence, whether within the particular experience focused on one as victim or offender. The inclusion of male research participants introduced a new dimension to the project and emphasised the need for reflexivity throughout the research process. Qualitative data collection methods were essential here in enabling me to be flexible and to accommodate my growing understanding of the meanings of violence for men. I was far less ready to assume 'understanding' of male speech and meanings, and male research participants were far more ready to correct my misapprehensions, than female research participants were. This highlighted the need to be open to difference with both male and female research participants and undoubtedly aided the production of more accurate and questioning social research. Other factors highlighted by the introduction of male research participants were the development of rapport, and issues of self-disclosure (Owen, 1995). The inclusion of male research participants definitely encouraged reflexivity on my part. Qualitative research methods were the only ones really capable of exploring in-depth the connected and contrasting experiences men and women have of violence.

**Studying men and violence**

This chapter is concerned with contrasting these male experiences with those of women. In particular, it focuses on the strategies victims adopt to deal with experiences of violence, and importantly, strategies for dealing with anxieties around violence. This section argues that violence is a relatively accepted part of men's lives, whilst it does not fit so readily into our conceptions of womanhood. In contrast, victim status is associated relatively easily with being a woman, whilst it conflicts with hegemonic conceptions of manhood. A consideration of strategies for dealing with fears of violences and experiences of violence itself, illustrate the main argument of the chapter. There are a wider range of less limiting strategies available for men to use in controlling anxieties about, and experiences of, violence.

Many commentators have considered the fear of crime phenomenon (for example Clemente & Kleiman, 1977; Garofalo, 1981; Hanmer &

Saunders, 1983; Stanko, 1985 and 1988; Young, 1988). They highlight the apparent anomaly between women's (and the elderly's) high fear of crime in the face of statistics which declare young men as those at greatest risk. In line with the majority of research on victimization which pays little attention to the experiences of (particularly young) men, research on fear of crime has concentrated on the discrepantly high fear of women, rather than the equally discrepant, low fear of men. The majority of explanations for this lack of anxiety on the part of men tend to see it as a simple function of *maschismo* culture (Young, 1988); a concern with masculine 'front'. Stanko & Hobdell (1993) suggest that to accept this explanation is to place too unquestioning a reliance on cultural stereotypes of hegemonic masculinity. Young (1988) notes that this lack of expression of fear may indeed reflect a lack of importance attached to the experience by men and not simply a reluctance to express fear.

For men, violence is a potentially less threatening experience, because violence itself is not considered so alien or separate from the everyday male (especially young male) life. Violence is viewed by many (men and women) as a more natural part of men's lives than women's and may thus be less fear inducing in anticipation. Many men view violence as involving more of an element of choice than women do, and to be more mutual. Violence is also often imagined to have fewer potential harmful consequences for men than for women.

Victim-blaming is a common strategy for dealing with violence and fears around it. Many victims also engage in self-blame in an attempt to limit anxieties about a reoccurrence of the violent event/s (Heath, 1984; Perloff, 1983). I argue that self and victim blaming are strategies engaged in more effectively by men than by women. This is because, for women, self (or victim) blame is associated with a more fixed identity or set of characteristics rather than, as is the case for many men, a transient identity or set of behaviours. Behavioural self-blame: 'may constitute an effective coping strategy because it helps survivors feel a sense of control over their own lives and provides strategies for avoiding revictimization' (Garnets, Herek & Levy, 1992, p.209; see also Lurigio and Resick, 1990). In contrast, characteristic self-blame can have very negative consequences, making victim-status seem inescapable, and violence appear significantly personal. If an individual considers that victimization follows who you are and not what you do, this can have a number of implications for both dealing with experiences of such violence, and anxieties about any potential victimization. There are obvious problems if the victim stereotype cannot be separated or distinguished from one's own characteristics. Many commentators have noted that being a woman is often seen to equate with being a victim, even:

> feminism sees the political situation of women as containing the possibility of victimization, because the seeds of victimization are inequality and the vulnerability produced by disadvantage

(Roberts, 1989, p.2).

As Roberts (1989) notes, although taking responsibility for victimization and feeling guilt is one way of regaining control of the situation, it often results in the victim personalising the violence with negative results (Lurigio and Resick, 1990). Ehrlich (1992) states that on average two and a half times more symptoms or psycho-physio stress indicators are suffered by victim's of ethno-violence (violence targeted at individuals on the basis of that individual's perceived membership of certain social groupings e.g. ethnicity) than victims whose victimization is not related to personal, socially inescapable characteristics.

Assuming that you are as un/likely as anyone else to be a victim (universal vulnerability, Perloff, 1983) being in a position to avoid characteristic self-blame is obviously easier for certain groups of people than it is for others. Many women experience victimization as a result of, or even as part of, being a woman, especially when the crime is one of sexual violence. The associations of violence with gender are often more complex and conflicting for male victims of violence. Violence may be viewed as part of being a man ('bearing injury like a man', Goldberg, 1979; 'taking part in masculine 'contests', Stanko & Hobdell, 1993; 'maintaining honour', Willis, 1990; 'negotiating a place in a hierarchy of oppression', Sawyer, 1974), but victimization is not. Victimization is often experienced as a direct affront to one's masculinity (Stanko, 1990; Stanko & Hobdell, 1993). Where victimization is associated with the masculine experience, it is often linked (and contained by this link) to a specific situation or time span (for example being a young man). In contrast, for men of colour, and to a certain extent, gay men, violence (and anxieties around it) may become more often associated with these identities, and not youthful-male ones.

Men are less likely to resist the term 'violence', than women are. This is perhaps because through a male frame, violence (even when experienced as a victim) can still be viewed in a positive light (Owen, 1995). Men can be gallant losers, having fought against the odds, and may even (in retrospect) wear injuries as trophies or war honours (Stanko & Hobdell, 1993). This re-framing of a negative experience is less available for women, whose achievement is often seen in terms of 'simply' surviving and regaining control of one's life. Thus for women, it is the aftermath that can be valued, but not the experience itself.

Whilst none of this is to suggest that being the victim of a violent experience is not a shattering experience for men, it does indicate that there are a wider range of positive coping behaviours available for men than for women. This also goes some way to explaining why women are more consciously and continually involved in daily negotiations of safety, whilst for men these are more closely linked to specific incidents of violence. So for men, experiences of violence can be redefined in a positive light or controlled by associating them with past behaviours or past identities in a way that is not available for women. The remainder of the chapter will concentrate on the differences between the association of transient young-male identities with violent victimization, in contrast with the association of a more fixed gender identity for women. It will be argued that in this way many men are able to contain anxieties and provide effective coping mechanisms for dealing with violent victimization. This can be done by relegating them to the past and by allocating themselves a more active, skilled role in the controlling any potential re-victimization.

**Contrasting expectations and experiences of violence: male and female talk**

The men involved in this study recognised that violence had played a part in their lives; for some it formed a more significant part than for others. Childhood and their school days was seen as the time when they began to learn about violence. For the women, from an early age, considerations of violence were clearly bound up with an awareness of personal safety and with victimization. Violence was something 'you just hoped ... wouldn't happen to you' (Jen). For the male participants violence was learnt about in a somewhat different context; through a different 'frame' (that of masculinity), (Stanko & Hobdell, 1993). Although all of the men had experienced potentially threatening experiences at a youthful age, discussions of violence set in this context focussed around the ways it could be used actively and to some extent positively; judging one's manhood, establishing one's position as a man. Violence is used as a way of establishing and negotiating hierarchies of power, it is: 'a way of establishing a hierarchy in a sense' (Andy); school was part of this process;

> There was definitely a pecking order amongst boys in secondary school, there was always fights between those at the top to get to the top of the pecking order
>
> (Phil).

Alex suggested that 'people work out a hierarchy quite early on'; Simon, that school fights 'were like playing a game'; Dave, that it was about establishing 'the law of the jungle'. However, this always leaves the possibility of ending up at the bottom of the heap, having difficulty in proving your masculinity:

> I felt insecure about it, inadequate, not complete, I didn't have the skill to be a hard man...I didn't particularly want to be, I just thought I ought to be
>
> (Owen).

For the women, these types of contests were clearly seen as a male preserve. As Sarah suggests 'it was just the lads going out to get the other lads to show they were hard'. In Jane's words 'just the boys being boys'. If a girl became involved it was seen as aberrant, sometimes amusing or somewhat embarrassing; definitely an unusual event, different from 'ordinary' or 'normal' male violence:

> there were fights between girls...sort of cat fights, you know, [laugh]... but that was more like a personal thing
>
> (Sarah).

Fighting between females was viewed by many of the women as the result of a personal project or conflict, not as it was for men, the result of a social one. Boys' fights revolved around a hierarchy; negotiating structured social positions. Girls fights were viewed as being concerned with personal issues; fallings out between friends, errant boyfriends, petty jealousies. Of course, these attitudes say much about the way in which activities women are involved in are viewed as less important, of lower status. Even when engaging in violence, women face the double standard of it being viewed as both less important (concerned with petty personal issues) and less serious; 'a bit of a joke really' (Jen); yet somehow becoming more punishable (unbefitting, unnatural). Whilst violence between boys was treated by school authorities as the (regrettable but inevitable) norm, violence between girls was punished as an unusual and especially deviant activity. However these attitudes are fostered, their effect is to normalise the presence of violence in many men's lives, and to emphasise that violence is alien and out of place in most women's lives.

Violence may be seen by men to be more than just a normal part of masculine experience, but also a way of proving one's masculinity, a badge of maleness. Willis (1990) talks of the way young men use violence to display hardness and honour. Stanko & Hobdell (1993) discuss the way men use violence as contests of masculinity. Harry (1992, p.115) notes that:

> adolescents are constantly mutually pressured to prove their commitment to the male gender role ... in the rather primitive eyes of the adolescent male, sexual and violent acts are the two main means through which they can prove their male commitment.

Violence is connected with manhood from an early age.

> Little boys learn the connection between violence and manhood very early in life ... They are encouraged to 'fight back', and bloodied noses and black eyes become trophies of their pint-sized virility
>
> (Donald, 1992 p.125).

Scars can become seen as status symbols. In this context,

> it was, like, a war honour, you know? ... I'm quite proud of having been through it now
>
> (Rob)

However traumatic and painful the physical and emotional effects of violence can be for men, there are still ways in which these very injuries can be used positively. This does not imply that men enjoy violent victimization, or that being physically injured does not bring a shocking sense of vulnerability. It does suggest that these experiences can be refigured in an honour gaining way. Injuries which may at first seen to demonstrate failure and diminish masculinity, can be used creatively to illustrate courage, honour and an essentially powerful masculinity. Many of the men interviewed, used examples of violent victimization where they had fought, or simply suffered, against the odds.

Unfair violence, in contrast to more 'mutual' fights, can be particularly disturbing. It does not offer the possibility that the now skilled individual could avoid or successfully negotiate a similar situation in the future.

However, in retrospect, it provides the victim with a potentially useful model; the gallant loser, the lone fighter against the odds. Thus the process and experience of the violent event itself can be controlled in this way:

> ... even at the time, like, I was thinking there's loads of them and just us two and I was scared ... we knew we were going to get the shit kicked out of us ... but it was funny ... a good story
>
> (Rob).

Models for female victims of violence, (almost always violence of this unfair, or unequal kind), are not so positive. Women are presented with models of feminine suffering and endurance. Positive attitudes focus not on any successful reframing of the event/s, but on surviving it; on dealing with the effects it may have on one's everyday life; on being 'normal' in spite of it:

> ... yes, it's had an enormous effect...and that sort of makes me angry ... but I'm pretty normal [laugh] ... I'm not giving him that
>
> (Louise).

Success is measured in terms of performance following, not during, the event/s:

> I was really scared ... [but] I don't want to give him that satisfaction [by changing daily patterns, by showing fear],
>
> (Karen).

Even when men experience violence of this unequal kind, many of them have greater access to strategies that can make this event less disempowering than women do. Of course, the majority of violent events experienced by most men are not so unequal and much more often involve only one incident (in contrast to womens experience). Violence against women is more largely perpetrated by someone in a structurally higher social position (i.e. a man) and is more likely to persist over a period of time. Perhaps as a consequence of this; as Young (1988) noted, much violence is often treated as trivial by young men. Very few of the men involved in this study saw violence of what they termed a 'mutual' nature as a serious event. 'it was play fighting, not really fighting' (Andy); just 'part of growing up ... no one really got hurt' (Dave); '[men hitting men] it's different isn't it to men hitting women...men hitting men its not part of the same thing' (Terry). Most men considered that the police would not treat violence between men as that serious either: 'they just went through the motions' (Steve).

Other research has supported this, particularly when violence occurs outside pubs or clubs (Corbett & Maguire, 1988). Similarly, adolescent and young male fights and violence associated (even expected) with(in) certain contexts were not treated with any degree of seriousness by the majority of the male research participants. Rob described it as; 'the sort of thing that used to happen quite a lot when I was a kid'. Steve associated it with youth 'gang mentality' engaged in by 'mostly younger men'. Terry described the centrality of violence in many young men's lives:

> I would say younger people are more violent ... on show and that, in pubs and football games ... [men] put themselves in [these] positions, it's part and parcel [of being a man].

In talking about football violence, Don stated:

> it's like other violence to men is, it's not serious to other males ... it 's like ritual ... testing yourself against peers.

Violence, then is acceptable if it is explained or contained within a particular context. As Greg put it, it would seem

> more serious if it happened out of context of the football ground ... you expect some sort of violence [there].

Violence can be made safe, or at least less threatening, if it is bounded within a particular context. These boundaries may be spatial, situational, or related to individual, physical markers (for example age). Potential anxieties about violence may be alleviated by containing violence within these boundaries. Some of the strategies are equally available to women, but again the range of strategies available to women is more limited and limiting. For example, however inaccurately, many women focus their anxieties around the threat of public violence from strange men. So they may as a result curtail their public behaviours to avoid this. They may also end up depending more heavily on those men more likely to be violent towards them (friends, lovers, husbands, colleagues etc., Harmer & Saunders, 1985). Men may more easily bound their experiences in a non- (or less) limiting manner. Some men experienced anxieties or violence in unfamiliar contexts or in context-bound situations: 'it happened when I used to go to clubs a lot' (Terry); 'this was all, like ten, fifteen years ago now' (Simon). However, because of the clear boundaries around these fear-inducing or violent situations, once home, or not in clubs, or older, these experiences do not create or maintain fears. In this way men are able to contain anxieties about past and potential future victimization by associating violence with particular contexts, particular parts/times of their lives. They are also able to separate these experiences from their current everyday lives by believing that they have since gained/developed skills that will enable them to a avoid a repeat of violent victimization. Andy considered he has gained 'danger perception skills'; Rob, had now ' become reasonably skilled at keeping out of fights'; Mike stated that he would not feel 'threatened now, I'm more experienced now, more wise and able to avoid [violence]'; Phil 'felt unsafe when I was younger in particular areas, at night, not now so much'; Steve stated 'I now feel relatively comfortable in sort of judging these sorts of situations'.

Women also refer to danger or violence managing skills that they feel they have developed:

> I probably wouldn't be such an easy object now
>
> (Jen, victim of sexual assault);

> ... as I got older. I began to realise there were some ways I could control it
>
> (Sarah, on her experiences of child sexual abuse).

As mentioned earlier, many of the opportunities women have for managing these anxieties about violence do involve characteristic self-blame or at the least a kind of behavioural self-blame that would involve them in placing quite significant restrictions on their behaviour. These strategies are also largely dependant on an avoidance of violence, rather than acknowledging any skills in dealing with any violent event itself. In contrast Stanko and Hobdell (1993) note the assumption that men can have no problems handling themselves in physical contests.

## Conclusion

Men's experiences of violence and the part it plays in their lives appears very different to that described by most women. When violence appears in women's lives it is almost always viewed as a disruption, a negative occurrence. It has no 'natural' role in women's lives (this is not implying that violence is not disruptive or negative in men's lives too, just that for women there is little potential for it to be viewed in any other, positive or normal light). Violence as experienced and feared by women is not so easily context-bound, by situation or age.

Violence is seen by many men (and women) to have a 'natural', and therefore less potentially threatening, place in young men's lives. When violence occurs in these situations, at this time in a man's life (adolescence through to early twenties) it is readily connected to male identity, to being a young man. In fact, these experiences of violence may even strengthen or be used later to define a sense of achieved masculinity. In contrast experiences of violence, at whatever age, are seen as a threatening experience for women. However much a real part of many women's lives, violence is still seen as somehow alien and separate from women's everyday experiences. Participating actively in violent encounters is especially viewed as in conflict with womanhood. Becoming a victim of violence does not appear to contradict ideas of femininity in the same way. Being labelled or feeling a victim of violence, at any age, can be a male-self threatening experience (Stanko, 1990; Stanko & Hobdell, 1993). Violence, although a relatively accepted or natural part of many men's lives becomes problematic when it becomes associated with 'failure'. The relationships between gender and violence do not appear to alter dramatically for most women whatever their age. In contrast, the experience and meaning of violence does change for many men depending upon their age.

Using qualitative methods of social research was a particularly powerful way to delve deep into these processes of created meaning. They were pertinent in exploring the active constructions of strategies for dealing with violence and the potential for violent victimization. This approach enabled the effect of the age of the participants, as well as their gender, to emerge from the data. Violence is a way through which many young men may prove or negotiate an achieved masculinity. Even victimization's traumatic and painful effects can be mediated by a language of courage and heroism for men. Age markers provide important and useful boundaries for men dealing with violence. Older men may not feel the need to engage in 'proving' activities to establish or retain status. They may not, by choice, be in situations where they consider violent encounters likely to occur. Older men also appear more confident that they have learnt skills that will enable them to avoid or negotiate their way out of violent situations. In contrast there is no comparable time period when violence is a 'normal' part of women's lives. For women there is no language to provide a successful or glamorous gloss to experiences of violence. There are no boundaries past which women may feel relatively safe from potential harm; except those which place limitations on their behaviour and social contact. It would be interesting to explore points beyond which men's identities as men, are affected by other identifications. These other identifications may result in the development of other, less successful, relationships between men and violence. One might speculate that significant other identities might be those attached to ethnic background, sexuality and old age. This might be compared to the way in which gay and black men are often viewed as 'legitimate' targets for violence (Stanko, 1990; Garnets, Herek & Levy, 1992). Ageing men perhaps begin to reach an age where the identity of 'victim' is no longer in conflict with their identities as men.

Essentially, the ability of men to avoid anxieties around safety and to deal with many experiences of violence, is bound up to their identities as men. An awareness of personal safety and potential victimization is for most women a routine part of being a woman. For certain men however, whilst violence might be routinized, this is not necessarily linked to a concept of victimization. Being a victim of violence might threaten one's masculinity, but when considering violence in general, men have many more options in defining their (potential) experiences in ways that are not necessarily negative. One of the most effective way of doing this is by associating violent experiences with a time when they more likely to encounter it, and were less skilled in dealing with it (i.e. their youth). Therefore, threats of violence are attached to a transient identity rather than a fixed identity of maleness.

## References

Aldridge, J. (1993), The textual disembodiment of knowledge in research account writing in sociology, *Sociology*, 27, (1), pp.53-66.

Clemente, F. & Kleiman, M.B. (1977), The fear of crime: causes and consequences, *Social Forces*, 56,(2), pp.519-531.

Connell, R. (1987), *Gender and power*, Stanford, Stanford University Press.

Connell, R. (1995) *Masculinities*, Cambridge, Polity Press.

Corbett, C. and Maguire, M. (1988), The value and limitations of victims support schemes, in Maguire, M. and Pointing, J. (eds), *Victims of crime: a new deal?*, Milton Keynes, Open University Press, pp.26-45.

Donald, R.R. (1992), Masculinity and machismo in Hollywood's war films in Craig, S. (ed.), *Men, masculinity and the media*, London, Sage. pp.124-136.

Ehrlich, H.J. (1992), The ecology of anti-gay violence in Herek, G.M. and Berrill, K.T. (eds), *Hate crimes, confronting violence against lesbians and gay men*, London, Sage. pp.105-112.

Garnets, L., Herek, G.M. and Levy, B. (1992), Violence and victimization of lesbians and gay men: mental health consequences in Herek, G.M. & Berrill, K.T. (eds), *Hate crimes: confronting violence against lesbians and gay men*, London, Sage, pp.207-226.

Garofalo, J. (1981), The fear of crime: causes & consequences, *Journal of Criminal Lawand Criminology*, 72, (2), pp.51-72.

Goldberg, H. (1979), *The new male: from self-destruction to self-care*, New York, Signet.

Hammersley, M. and Atkinson, P. (1983), *Ethnography: principles in practice*, London, Tavistock.

Hanmer, J. and Saunders, S. (1983), Blowing the cover of the protective male: a community study of violence to women in Garmamikow, E. *et al* (eds), *The public and the private* London, Heinemann, pp.28-46.

Harry, J. (1992), Conceptualizing anti-gay violence in Herek, G.M. and Berrill, K.T. (eds), *Hate crimes: confronting violence against lesbians and gay men*, London, Sage. pp.113-122.

Herek, G.M. and Berriil, K.T. (eds), *Hate crimes. confronting violence against lesbians and gay men*, London, Sage.

Heath, L. (1984), Impact of newspaper crime reports on fear of crime: multimethodological investigation, *Journal of Personal and Social Psychology* 47,(2), pp.263-276.

Jones, S. (1985), Depth interviewing in Walker, R (ed.), *Applied qualitative research*, Aldershot, Gower. pp.45-55.

Kelly, L. (1989), The continuum of sexual violence in Hanmer, J. & Maynard, M. (eds),*Women, violence and social control*, London, Macmillan. pp.46-60.

Laws, S. (1990), *Issues of blood.- The politics of menstruation*, London, Macmillan.

Lurigio, A.J. and Resick, P.A. (1990), Healing the psychological wounds of criminal victimization: predicting postcrime distress and recovery in Lurigio, A.J., Skogan, W.G. and Davis, R.C. (eds) (1990), *Victims of crime: problems, policies, and programs*, London, Sage. pp.28-40.

Morgan, D. (1990), Men, masculinity, and the process of social enquiry in Roberts, H. (ed), *Doing feminist research,* London, Routledge and Kegan Paul, pp.83-113.

Owen, J.M. (1995), Women-talk and men-talk: constructing and resisting victim status in R. Dobash, E. Dobash and L. Noaks (eds) *Gender and crime*, Cardiff, University of Wales Press, pp.246-268.

Perloff, L.S. (1983), Perceptions of vulnerability to victimsation *Journal of Social Issues* 39,(2), pp.41-62.

Ramazanoglu, C. (1992), On feminist methodology: male reason versus female empowerment *Sociology*, 26, (2), pp.207-212.

Reinhartz, S. (1992), *Feminist methods in social research*, Oxford, Oxford University Press.

Roberts, C. (1989), *Women and rape*, London, Harvester Wheatsheaf.

Sawyer, J. (1974) On male liberation in Pleck, J.H. and Sawyer, J. (eds), *Men, and masculinity,* New Jersey, Prentice Hall, Inc. pp.47-68.

Stanko, E. (1985), *Intimate intrusions*, London, Routledge.

Stanko, E. (1988), Hidden violence against women in Maguire, M. & Pointing, J. (eds), *Victims of crime- a new deal ?* Milton Keynes, Open University Press. pp.40-46.

Stanko, E. (1990), *Everyday violence: how women and men experience sexual and physical danger*, London, Pandora.

Stanko, E. and Hobdell, K. (1993), Assault on men: masculinity and male victimization in *British Journal of Criminology,* 1 (5) pp.400-415.

Stanley, L (1991), (ed.), *Feminist praxis: research, theory and epistemology in feminist sociology,* London, Routledge.

Stanley, L. and Wise, S. (1991), Methodology, methods and epistemology in Stanley, L (1991), (ed.), *Feminist praxis: research, theory and epistemology in feminist sociology*, London, Routledge. pp.20-62.

Willis, P. (1990), *Common culture: symbolic work at play in the everyday cultures of the young*, London, Milton Keynes.

Young, J (1988), Risk of crime and fear of crime: a realist critique of survey-based assumptions. in Maguire, M. & Pointing, J. (eds), *Victims of crime: a new deal?* Milton Keynes, Open University Press. pp.164-176.

# 5 Chance to choice: Two generations of reproductive decision making

## A study of a group of mothers and daughters with Duchenne Muscular Dystrophy in the family

*Evelyn P. Parsons*

### Introduction

> You see the thing is with my generation we have got the opportunity of having the sex test and finding out whether it's a boy or a girl, whereas my mother didn't, she was straight in you have a boy or a girl and that's that.... that's one thing we have gained out of all of this.
>
> (Ros Hughes Daughter 1b)

This is how Ros Hughes described the difference between her mother's experience and her own. Ros had a brother with the genetic disease, Duchenne Muscular Dystrophy (Duchenne) and she was potentially a carrier of the defective gene associated with the disease. When she became pregnant she had fetal sexing by amniocentesis (a prenatal test carried out between 16 and 18 weeks of pregnancy) and decided to abort a male fetus. Three years later her second pregnancy was tested, during the tenth week, by means of chorion villus sampling. CVS is a pre-natal test usually performed in the tenth-twelfth week of pregnancy. It involves removing cells from the choronic villi for the detection of chromosomal abnormalities, or DNA analysis for genetic disorders. Over a period of some 25 years this family's reproductive history has reflected the changes that have taken place in medical technology. The contrasting experience of a group of mothers and daughters will be explored in this chapter, drawing on their own accounts. I will explore how technology has changed the whole context of women's reproductive decision making. The 1960s saw the introduction of fetal sexing by amniocentesis and the legalisation of abortion, whilst the 1980s saw the development of CVS and increasingly sophisticated DNA analysis. These have all been portrayed as 'advances', which immediately implies positive progress, but is that the case? This chapter will explore the implications for a group of women who, because of a particular genetic mutation in their family, find that their reproductive decision making is dominated by modern medical technology.

**The study and its background**

Duchenne is a lethal genetic disease which affects boys, but is carried by non-manifesting females. Boys are normal at birth and only begin to show signs of muscle weakness when they are 3-4 years old. They usually become wheelchair bound when they are 10-11 years old and rarely live to celebrate their 21st birthday. In every pregnancy, carrier women face a 50/50 chance that the faulty gene will be transmitted: in the case of a boy he will manifest the physical symptoms of Duchenne, whilst a girl becomes, like her mother, a carrier. It was during the 1960s that the first amniocentesis tests were offered to ascertain whether women were carrying a male fetus, but at that stage there was little certainty as to their specific carrier risks. Many women, in an attempt to avoid an affected boy, were terminating all male pregnancies, many of whom would have been perfectly healthy. Information about carrier risks became more reliable with the introduction of creatine kinase carrier testing (CK), but again women were making decisions on the basis of risk figures. It was during the 1980s that CVS became available, and with the cloning of the Duchenne gene, by the end of that decade, women could be given more reliable information about their carrier status and the condition of their fetus.

During the 1980s I initiated a sociological study to explore the experience of women who had lived with Duchenne in their family. To enable comparisons between two generations (in particular the different social and medical context of their genetic decision making), the sample was specifically structured to include both mothers and daughters. In total 54 women met the criteria for inclusion and agreed to join the study. This represented 22 mothers and 32 daughters. The definition of 'mother' was based on women having an affected son and that of 'daughter' on a women's sibling relationship to an affected boy.

The alternatives within sociology between the quantitative methodologies with fixed schedules and structured interviews and the qualitative, have been widely debated (Glaser and Strauss 1967; van Maanen 1983; Lofland and Lofland 1984; Strauss 1987; Hammersley 1992;

Hammersley 1993; Hammersley and Atkinson 1995). The linear, deductive generation of quantitative data contrasts sharply with qualitative material which emerges, Agar (1980) argues, from a continual dialectic between data and analysis, experience and interpretation. It is rooted in a sociology of social interaction which focuses on the point where meanings and definitions are constructed. There were five main reasons why a qualitative methodology was adopted in this research. First, it was clear that the subject matter was too fragile to expose to the exactitudes of a quantitative survey. Experiences of living with a terminal childhood disease and genetic decision making under conditions of uncertainty were not topics which readily fitted into neat, pre-prescribed categories. Graham (1984) refers to this more informal method of data collection as 'surveying through stories'; the narrative being the ideal methodological catalyst which places experiences in their biographical context. She argues that structured research tools fracture women's lives and '... aspects of our social life which cannot be shaped into answer-sized pieces are inevitably lost to posterity' (Graham 1984 p.119).

Second, I was concerned to explore those issues the women found important rather than impose a rigid structure on the encounter. Lofland and Lofland (1984) argue that the structured interview determines the frequency of preconceived things, whilst the unstructured seeks to find out what kind of things exist in the first place. Third, the informal interview gives respondents control over the extent emotional issues are explored. As Graham (1984 p.120) argues 'The story marks the boundaries of what the individual is prepared to tell...it provides the teller with a way of controlling the release of information about herself'. Fourth, adopting a qualitative approach allows unanticipated responses to emerge and become incorporated into the research which is continuously reflexive. Finally, the qualitative interview enables respondents time to cope with topics which are rarely verbalised. Murcott (1987) refers to the interview as the occasion for thinking consciously about matters otherwise taken for granted.

The qualitative interview context therefore was conceived as a social occasion with its own unique context and setting. Each person bringing to it their particular stocks of knowledge, their personal biography and specific expectations. It is unrealistic to claim that the interviews were totally unstructured because the women knew I wanted to talk about living with Duchenne and that an outline agenda had been set. It was in such informal, in-depth interviews that the women talked about their reproductive decision making and their response to technological change. The reproductive experience of the majority of the mothers had predated new technology, whilst the daughters' spanned the whole spectre of technological change from the 1960s to the mid 1980s. There were clear differences between the two generations studied. The introduction of carrier testing and fetal sexing by amniocentesis or CVS, combined with the increasing availability of genetic counselling and the growing social acceptability of abortion, have progressively created reproductive options not available to women before the 1960s. The daughters' accounts were stories of choice, whilst the mothers' were tales of chance. Subject to consent all the interviews were tape-recorded and later transcribed. Throughout the text all names are pseudonyms and a family reference number is given so that the mother/daughter relationship can be recognised.

## Reproductive chances: A generation of mothers

*Mothers' experience*

There were 22 respondents in the study who were mothers and they all described their reproductive experience in terms of chance. Mrs Poole said:

> You know with us, you just had them and it was a handicap and that was just too bad, you ... just had to accept it sort of thing. Nowadays they have got a choice.
>
> (Mrs Poole, Mother 26)

Their 66 pregnancies (26 affected boys, 5 unaffected boys and 35 females) had all occurred prior to the introduction of prenatal fetal sexing. For the majority (15 mothers) their family building was completed before the diagnosis had been made, the remainder revised their plans deciding to have no more children. Mrs Harvey had wanted four children but when the diagnosis on John had been made she and her husband decided:

> ... not to risk any more 'cause we don't think it's fair on the children. In them days they didn't do any tests, in fact they didn't do anything about it at all.
>
> (Mrs Harvey, Mother 2)

For Mrs Read it was not worth the chance:

> I don't think it would be fair to have another one like Timothy, I wouldn't take a chance that it might be a little girl, you know, I would be too afraid.
>
> (Mrs Read, Mother 8)

Five mothers were actually pregnant when their sons were first diagnosed as having Duchenne. Mrs Skinner and Mrs Taylor felt that at that time there was nothing they could do about it:

> I mean there was no question of abortion you just went ahead, you know and just prayed every night that it was going to be a girl.
>
> (Mrs Skinner, Mother 15)

> But when they told me about Mark having Duchenne I was already seven months pregnant with Roy so I couldn't do anything about it
>
> (Mrs Taylor, Mother 3)

Two mothers opted for unsexed terminations:

> Just after Conrad was diagnosed I found I was pregnant, how on earth I just do not know because I was on the pill, I suppose my body was very low, so I had ... (voice faded avoiding using the words) ... it was done quick, I didn't have time to think about it... it was just too much of a risk. Yes it would have been too much of a risk. Well after that I was sterilised. I didn't want to be at all but you couldn't have another child like that.
>
> (Mrs Jarvis, Mother 24)

> The thing was I got pregnant and I went to the doctor and told him that I couldn't go through all that again, it could have been a boy. I just couldn't have coped with another one. The thought of bringing another child into the world knowing that that child is not going to live and is going to suffer, to me it is cruel.
>
> (Mrs Wiggan, Mother 27)

The fifth one - Mrs Talbot was against abortion. Mrs Wiggan went on to describe how traumatised she had been as a result of her termination:

> I was terrible after it, for about 6 months after I was really bad, it kept playing on my mind, I know everyone is different.
>
> (Mrs Wiggan, Mother 27)

There was one conviction that ran through the majority of the mothers' accounts:

> If I had known I wouldn't have had any children
>
> (Mrs Brown, Mother 1)

> As far as having children, Oh No, [said emphatically], oh no I wouldn't have them. You know they walk up to a certain age and that's it.
>
> (Mrs Taylor, Mother 3)

> If I had known the risks I was taking I would never have had them because I don't think it is fair. I would rather have had none at all.
>
> (Mrs Downs, Mother 11)

> I don't think I would ever have had children
>
> (Mrs Wiggan, Mother 27)

They would rather have been without children than see their son suffer, as one mother said 'it just tears you apart inside'.

*Mothers' attitudes to the new technology*

The advent of the new technology was something that all the mothers knew about because of their daughter's involvement. For some there was considerable regret that it had not come sooner:

> That's the first thing I would ask for is the tests ... I would definitely have the tests ... they do make a lot of difference. Well I mean the girls today it does give them a better chance, you know, with us you just had them ... I would definitely have them and if they told me it was a boy I would have ... (lowered her voice) ... if they would have said it was a boy I would have said: 'No that's it' ... I wouldn't like to see another child having to go through what David had to go through.
>
> (Mrs White, Mother 4)

> No, I mean I would take advantage of the tests that Belinda can have to sex the child for a start and I think if I had found

out it was a boy, if I could have known when I was pregnant that it was a boy or a girl that would have put a lot of my fears to rest. As it was I just had to wait. I don't think I could have coped with two, I mean I admire people that have got two boys with dystrophy, how they cope I don't know.

(Mrs Skinner, Mother 15)

If I was having a child now and it was a boy and they said he would be all right I would have it but if they said he had Duchenne that would be it, I don't think it's right.

(Mrs Wiggans, Mother 27)

For others there was a high degree of ambivalence and it was a decision they were glad they had not had to face. When I asked Mrs Williams whether she would have considered prenatal testing had it been available she was very hesitant:

... Um ... I don't know ... because it didn't happen to me did it? You can't look at it like that, we loved Keith and we had a lot of pleasure out of him so you really can't say. I think it's all to easy to say 'Of course I wouldn't have a termination', I don't like the thought of abortion anyway but I think ... um ... I don't really know ... it is difficult to say ... it's not an easy thing.

(Mrs Williams, Mother 18)

No I am glad I didn't have a decision to make ... I'm against abortion, you know for just for abortions sake but ... er ... I don't know whether I could consciously bring another child into the world, as I said I wouldn't like to be in the position where I would have to make that decision. I just don't know what I would do.

(Mrs Roper, Mother 25)

The thing is a lot of people say to you 'Oh God if I had known I was going to have a handicapped baby there is no way I would have it' but having gone through it ... you see he was very easy ... there was no way of him not being ... (mumbling under her breath) ... I think about the thought of having aborted Nick ... of him not being (voice faded)

(Mrs Griffiths, Mother 26)

*Mother's messages*

A daughter's inheritance from her mother was not only genetic (she too could be carrying the Duchenne gene) but also social. It was clear that it was mothers who took the responsibility for information management - what daughters were told, both about their brother's disease and their own potential carrier status, and its implications. In fact mothers were sometimes used by daughters to break the news to potential partners: 'I left him with mother to give him the low down' (Abigail Hayward - Daughter 3a). It is not surprising to learn that the nature of the communication between mother and daughter was very different from family to family and was influenced by a mother's own experience and perspective. There were those mothers who, inspite of knowing about the new technology, were anxious that their daughters did not repeat their experience. Mrs Bevan said 'I wouldn't like her [Lucy] to go through what I've been through', although she did acknowledge '..it's her life, it's up to her, I can't tell her what to do'. But mother's messages were clearly recorded and remembered. Sally's mother had told her that the only answer was not to have any children:

> I think she had this fear you see when she was having children there wouldn't have been a lot she could do about it, so she had this fear that the easiest thing is 'Don't have children'. She used to make it sound so black, 'It would be better for you not to have children, you just don't know it could happen and it's best not to'.
>
> (Sally Abbott, Daughter 16a)

Mrs Skinner was also cautious, warning Belinda that if there was any doubt she should say 'No' and they should not have any children. In her opinion they would not cope with an affected boy: 'it wouldn't be fair to her, her husband and I don't think her in-laws could take it'. Abigail Hayward had been quite optimistic following genetic counselling, but her mother reiterated caution:

> Don't listen to that, you're a carrier and that's that. You're a carrier so don't get your hopes up.
>
> (Abigail Hayward, Daughter 3a)

For Mrs Cope the only answer was to wait and see because she felt that progress would be made both in terms of more accurate carrier testing and treatments for the disease:

> I keep trying to drum into them [Gillian and Penny] to wait for a bit. You see Gillian wants a baby but I keep saying 'they're nearly having the breakthrough so just wait'. She can at least wait another two years.
>
> (Mrs Cope, Mother 6)

Other mothers were instrumental in ensuring their daughters kept in touch with the Department of Genetics, both for carrier testing and any prenatal screening. Mrs Brown said:

> I hated the thought of doing what I did, making sure that they knew, you have always got this thing on your mind but the thing is they have got the choice. I remember one day Hilda said to me 'Mum when I get married if I have a child like that it won't make a difference to me' and I said 'Hilda you must never ever think like that because when you have actually got it it tears you apart inside'. There is no way I would want a child to go through it.
>
> (Mrs Brown, Mother 1)

This group of mothers had lived for many years with the responsibility of caring for a son with Duchenne and the knowledge that they may also have passed the defective gene to their daughter. They were women who had had very little choice in their reproductive patterning. As Mrs Griffiths said, the key difference between her having Nick and her daughter having a son was that she had not done it 'knowingly'. All the daughters in the study were aware of their risks, and that awareness brought with it a responsibility for their reproductive decision making. Their experiences will be explored in the next section.

## Reproductive choices: A generation of daughters

The generation of daughters who were part of this study had knowledge about their potential carrier status and reproductive options that their mothers would never have dreamt medically possible or socially acceptable. For these women fetal sexing was available, by either amniocentesis or CVS, and for those pregnant during the 1980s the choices they made were based on increasingly accurate risk analysis. (It should be noted that the more recent innovations of prenatal diagnosis by family deletion analysis or prenatal exclusion testing were not available at the time the fieldwork was carried out between 1986-1987).

It is important however to set the daughters' accounts of their reproductive choices in the context of current debates about prenatal screening and genetic counselling. Traditional approaches have left these domains to the medical profession, accepting their reassurances that each intervention would only be undertaken in the best interest of the patient and the extent of information given a matter of 'reasonable judgement' (Wald and Law 1992). More recently writers have been asking structural questions about the nature of informed consent in a society where medicine and technology are so highly valued. Is non-directive counselling possible (Clarke 1991)? Are women aware that prenatal screening is an option not an obligation (Clarke and Parsons 1992)? Can it be argued that genetic counselling has developed in recent years as the result of increasing public demand for information and preventive services, or is it, as Yoxen (1982) claims, part of a professional conspiracy that acts as a respectable cover for a new eugenics?

> Over the past thirty years a small group ... has been able to exploit the medical opportunities offered by an 'emergent' group of diseases. They now offer specialist advice to increasing numbers of people in counselling clinics.
>
> (Yoxen, 1982, p.152-153)

Farrant (1985), in her study of amniocentesis and the politics of prenatal screening argues genetic counselling is biased because of its political motivation and cultural definition. It reinforces a dominant ideology that poses solutions to disability in terms of medical science and maternal responsibility rather than social and political change:

> At all stages of screening, counselling is systematically biased towards encouraging women to take up the tests and to have abortions if an abnormality is detected, rather than providing women with the information and support to make informed choices and to avoid unnecessary distress.
>
> (Farrant, 1985, p.110)

Like other feminist writers Farrant doubts the authenticity of the claims that advances in reproductive technology herald increasing choice for women:

> The concept of 'choice' about amniocentesis ... needs to be located within the context of ante-natal care which generally provides women with very little control over decisions about their own treatment.
>
> (Farrant, 1985, p.113)

Rothman (1987) similarly argues that there is only choice for those who want what society wants:

> The new technology ... offers new choices but it also creates new structures and new limitations on choice.
>
> (Rothman, 1987, p.14)

> In gaining the choice to control the quality of our children, we may rapidly lose the choice not to control the quality, the choice of simply accepting them as they are.
>
> (Rothman, 1987, p.11)

Whatever the arguments about the underlying motivation for screening one thing is very clear: the change from reproductive chance to reproductive choice has given women a new responsibility for the health of their fetus. When there was no knowledge of risk, the arrival of a disabled child was seen as something beyond personal control. This is not so for this generation of daughters: the new technology has brought choice and created a climate in which the ultimate responsibility for a disabled child can no longer be externalised. It is a matter of personal liability.

> Blame begins to insinuate itself. The birth of a severely disabled child, when the disability could have been prenatally diagnosed and the pregnancy terminated begins to be seen as an act of irresponsibility. The standards of production rise and we are held accountable by those standards.
>
> (Rothman, 1987, p.227)

New reproductive technology brings with it new levels of knowledge and awareness which in turn begin to infiltrate and change definitions in society as to the nature of responsible parenthood. The question the rest of this chapter will address is: how do a group of women describe their experience of the new technology when they have lived with a genetic disease in the family, something the majority of their mothers would have chosen to avoid had they been born in a later generation.

During the course of the study 32 daughters were interviewed, all of whom were aware of their carrier status, but only 22 of them had actually made a reproductive decision. It is these women's accounts of their 40 pregnancies that will be reported here. The remaining 10 daughters discussed the issues of prenatal testing and abortion but their responses were purely hypothetical. There were two options open to women who were aware of their risk: they could family build without medical intervention, that is they could become 'risk takers' or they could be 'risk refusers' by opting for fetal sexing or having an unsexed termination. Of the 40 conceptions on 19 occasions the women were risk takers and on 21 occasions they were risk refusers. The majority of women showed reproductive consistency. That was, in each of their pregnancies they followed the same pattern of decision making, 8 women were risk takers with 14 pregnancies and 9 women were risk refusers with 12 conceptions. There were however 5 women who appeared in both groups because with 5 pregnancies they were risk takers and with 9 pregnancies they were risk refusers. In terms of this generation the important question to ask is what factors influenced some women to reject the opportunity of medical intervention and some to accept?

*Risk takers: the daughters who refused testing*

There were five reasons given by the daughters for not taking up the offer of prenatal testing. First, there were those who defined their risk as being too low to warrant intervention. Sheila Keats had a carrier risk of around 1% and she said:

> It didn't really concern me because I had had the blood tests
> [CK carrier testing] and they had said that it was very, very,
> low risk ... it didn't really strike me that if it was a little boy
> that it might have muscular dystrophy.
>
> (Sheila Keats, Daughter 14b)

Joan White, Irene Corke and Anne Silcox all told a similar story. They had taken the decision that at their levels of risk testing was of no value because they would not abort a male fetus.

Secondly, there were women who, regardless of their level of risk, found abortion unacceptable:

> My husband we sat down and talked about it ... if we knew it was a boy or a girl I wouldn't go and have an abortion anyway, whether it was handicapped or not ... if you have an abortion you're still taking that life, you're not giving that child a chance.
>
> (Millie Murray, Daughter 21a)

> They asked me if I wanted tests and I said 'No' - well I knew there was no point I knew I couldn't go through with an abortion.
>
> (Kitty Bain, Daughter 12a)

This awareness about the potential health of the fetus, and concern about 'not giving the child a chance', was echoed in other accounts; and constitutes the third reason the daughters gave for being risk takers.

> The thing is they can't really tell you whether it is definitely affected or not, whether I was carrying a baby with muscular dystrophy or not, it may be, it all boils down to my own decision whether I want to risk the fact that it may or may not be.
>
> (Laura Coles, Daughter 16b)

Laura went on to give another reason for her decision to refuse testing:

> No, because I mean, he (her brother) made it worth while really ... because I know what my brother was like ... you've always got that at the back of your mind, you could be getting rid of somebody like him again.
>
> (Laura Coles, Daughter 16b)

The fourth reason the women gave was their over-riding desire for a child. For these women it was a chance worth taking:

> When I was having my first baby I didn't go and have any tests, I think perhaps it was stupid but I would have terminated a perfectly healthy pregnancy, someone must have been looking over me but the thing was ... (long pause)

... well, because after all I think most women want a child even if it's the only one.

(Mandy Farmer, Daughter 19a)

If I had gone through an abortion it's easy to say 'you can try again' but I knew the reality was that I wouldn't have tried again ... I had to make my mind up - not the fact of whether it was right to take the baby away or not, but whether I could have no children at all ... that was the decision ... Yes, I mean, my selfish desire to have a baby really ... it was me specifically that wanted a baby ...

(Kitty Bain, Daughter 12a)

The final factor that had influenced two of the women was their previous experience of prenatal testing and a termination. Julia Charles had three pregnancies, on the first she had amniocentesis and terminated a male fetus but her negative experience made her decide against testing on her two subsequent pregnancies:

No I couldn't have gone through all that again. No I said if it's a boy I'll have it. I didn't mind the pain or anything like that but I was nearly five months pregnant and I had to go through the birth and everything like that, it was dreadful, it was awful. I couldn't go through that again, I regretted it ... (pause) ... deep down I know I've done the right thing, but I have always regretted it.

(Julia Charles, Daughter 6b)

This group of daughters, regardless of their potential carrier risks, took the decision to avoid medical intervention. For them the cost was too high. They each had their own specific reasons for why they would prefer to face the future with an affected son rather than have a termination. The outcomes of those 19 pregnancies were 2 affected boys, 8 unaffected boys and 9 girls. It is interesting to compare the response of this group with those who opted for medical intervention. There were cases where women, with similar risk levels, followed very different decision patterns. For example with a risk of under 1% Joan White was a risk taker but Belinda Tyson was a risk refuser. The significance of women's own definition of their risk liability was evidently more important than its actual mathematical level. Levels of carrier risk liability are not the only factor in determining the uptake of testing (Parsons and Atkinson 1992; Parsons and Atkinson 1993; Parsons and Clarke 1993).

*Risk refusers: the daughters who opted for testing*

There were 9 daughters (12 pregnancies) who were consistent risk refusers, and a further 5 women who changed their pattern of decision making to become risk refusers on 9 of their pregnancies. Of these 21 pregnancies, 16 were fetally sexed and 5 were terminated prior to fetal sexing. For Sue her first two pregnancies had been sexed by amniocentesis and had been girls, but her third pregnancy she defined differently:

> When they told me I was pregnant I had a termination, I was terrified, in my mind I was going to have a baby with muscular dystrophy ... it was in my mind that it was a boy. I sort of knew because I was ill with the other two, this time there was no sickness, it was like a change of pregnancy, change of sex you know,
>
> (Sue Black, Daughter 5b)

Sue faced no ethical dilemma about having an abortion:

> I think it's all right (abortion) you either have the heart-ache then or have a deeper one later like. I mean if they are not born then they are better off.
>
> (Sue Black, Daughter 5a)

Neither did Rebecca:

> Not that we agree on abortion, but it's three lives you are playing with ... no because you know from the moment that you have got him you are on borrowed time ... it's awful to see someone, normal in every other way deteriorating.
>
> (Rebecca Green, Daughter 2a)

The women gave two main reasons for their decision to be risk refusers. First, women who were risk refusers, irrespective of their actual mathematical level of carrier risk defined it as 'too high'. Jessica Firth (Daughter: 20a) told me: 'It was just too much of a risk, the risks were just too high ...'. For Belinda Tyson (Daughter 15a) even a 1% risk was more than she was prepared to take.

The second reason given for accepting technological intervention was their prior biographical experience. They talked in terms of life being 'too hard' and how the whole family 'suffers' as a result:

I experienced it [living with her brother] so there is no way I
would want a child to go through it.

(Hilda James, Daughter 1a)

I've got to be quite honest with you I was quite bitter about
my brother ... I have seen what my mother and father have
been through. No I don't think, I know we couldn't go
through with it.

(Jean Moffoot, Daughter 28a)

I just know I wouldn't be strong enough to go through it a
second time

(Rebecca Green, Daughter 2a)

Sue Black was quite determined not to take any risks:

I saw my mother going through it, I know it sounds hard, but
I wouldn't have took the chance ... because I had the choice
there was no way I was going to have the life my mother
had.

(Sue Black, Daughter 5b)

For women who were risk refusers their definition of 'responsible
behaviour' was framed in terms of utilising the new reproductive
technology and 'having all the tests':

But I think to myself if you are lucky enough to have the test
you should go ahead, I think it is unfair to the child and the
family.

(Gail Broad, Daughter 7a)

I was just so lucky that I could have the earlier test, but it
really is the only sensible thing to do.

(Gillian Lilley, Daughter 6a)

This contrasts with the definitional construction of risk takers for whom
'responsible behaviour' was seen in terms of 'giving the fetus a chance' by
refusing medical intervention.

For some couples, having opted for testing, their final decision was
clear cut:

> It was something we came to before we married ... we knew
> what the chances were when we went into it and we have a
> good talk ... we said that if it was a boy we would terminate.
>
> (Janet Hargreaves, Daughter 5a.)

For others there was a high degree of ambivalence. Technology was available but they recognised that for them it carried a cost:

> I had the tests not really thinking of the fact that I might
> have to face the chance of not having a little girl.
>
> (Ros Hughes, Daughter 1b)

It was the same for Jean Moffoot. She and her husband had originally decided against having children but in time changed their minds. They had made no decision about what to do if the amniocentesis result was male. Their recipe was 'just to live from day to day'. They talked about their experience.

> We had to wait three weeks and that was sheer ... well ...
> nerve racking. I don't know but that put me right off ... it
> was a hell of a worry. It had built up from the time I knew
> that I was having the baby, it was such a worry.
>
> (Jean Moffoot, Daughter 28a)

Her husband joined in:

> I will never forget it, I was trying to be supportive to her as
> well but thinking the worst myself, if it went the wrong way,
> to have to have it terminated ... I tell you what it was, people
> were saying: 'Congratulations' when she was pregnant, we
> were thinking of whether we could have it or not. It was at
> the back of your mind all the time, you couldn't get too
> excited or involved because - that was the worst part of it.

Rothman (1987) describes this experience as the 'tentative pregnancy'; a period in the pregnancy when a woman is waiting in limbo, unsure whether she is a mother or just the carrier of a defective fetus. Jean and her husband were fortunate, they had a little girl. It was however this experience of the new technology that made them decide against having any more children:

> I just know I couldn't have gone through with trying for
> another knowing that it would have been a boy, it would
> have had a real effect on my husband having to terminate a
> son, I don't think I could have, the strain would have been a
> bit too much.

For them prenatal testing was part of being responsible parents and they felt
the cost was too high.

Of the 16 pregnancies that were tested 7 were by amniocentesis and 9
by CVS. There was only one situation where amniocentesis was chosen
once CVS was available, this was because a daughter had lost a female
fetus following CVS. The assumption is made that CVS is less stressful
than amniocentesis because it can be done earlier, the results do not take as
long and any termination can be done during the first trimester (Green
1994). The evidence from this group of women would support these
assumptions.

> I had an amniocentesis then I had a termination because they
> said it was a boy but I was nearly 5 months ... I had to go
> through the birth and everything like that it was dreadful, it
> was awful.
>
> (Gillian Lilley, Daughter 5a)

> I was just black and blue after the amniocentesis ... I was so
> bruised, I had scars for months.
>
> (Abigail Hayward, Daughter 3a)

One daughter who had experienced both tests was in no doubt:

> Oh yes I did prefer it (CVS), that amnio., that was terrible,
> very ... it disturbed me a lot, psychologically it did, terrible
> ...
>
> (Ros Hughes, Daughter 1b)

Penny Long, like other women, felt that the earlier CVS meant she
could have the result before her pregnancy became public knowledge:

> You see no-one needs to know, you know, you can just slip
> off and no-one really knows.
>
> (Penny Long, Daughter 6b)

I suppose you know you're pregnant yourself, but nobody else does and if something goes wrong, whatever ... you're the only one that is going to have to carry that around with you.

(Janet Hargreaves, Daughter 5b)

Those women who had had an amniocentesis were reluctant to repeat their experience and found the much earlier CVS more acceptable. It is important to recognise, as Green (1994) points out, that there is still very little data to support the assumption that the psychological impact of terminations after CVS is necessarily any less traumatic.

This group of daughters were the first generation offered the choice of prenatal testing on the basis of increasing certainty in carrier risk information. Their reproductive lives had spanned the introduction of amniocentesis and the early days of CVS but it will be their daughters who will be offered, for the first time, certainty in early fetal analysis.


**Conclusion**

This study has captured the very different reproductive experience of a group of women as it has changed between two generations; a result of both changes in reproductive technology and social norms and values. The stories the women told were indeed far too fragile and too unique to have been exposed to the exactitudes of a structured questionnaire. There were occasions when some of the women were prepared, using the vehicle of their own biography, to talk about emotional issues in a depth no interviewer would have dared to impose. The structured interview would not have caught, the richness, nor the fine graining of the women's lives. Life, for them, on the cutting edge of Duchenne was not a question of facts and figures but a matter of individual experience and definition. Although the majority of mothers talked very positively about the new reproductive technology that had missed their generation not all their daughters did, in practice, opt for medical intervention. They had all lived with the same genetic disease in the family and were offered reproductive choice and yet women with comparable levels of mathematical risk adopted very different patterns of reproductive behaviour. To assume, as some radical writers do, that all women are dominated by the new technology and thereby fail to exercise choice is too simplistic. A recent analysis of women's reproductive patterning over a period of 25 years in Duchenne has demonstrated that technology does influence reproductive patterns, in that with increasing levels of certainty and reducing levels of invasive testing there is an increase in women's willingness to have prenatal testing. The correlation is not direct, a number of other variables are operating. Preliminary evidence from the all-Wales newborn screening programme for Duchenne is confirming that even when an index case is identified, and prenatal testing possible, not all families opt for medical intervention. The choices available to women are inevitably structured by the medical technology available and the nature and structuring of the information they are given, but it has been seen from this study that women constructed very different reproductive biographies in the face of similar structural constraints. Their unique stories illustrate the importance of individual definitions:

> Each individual comes into the situation with a different train of experience a different outlook or perspective, and this in turn becomes a factor in the total situation, leading to different 'definitions' of the situation and subsequently to different behaviour.
>
> (Thomas, 1937, p.7)

### References

Agar, M. (1980), *The professional stranger.* New York , Academic Press

Clarke, A.J. (1991), Is non-directive genetic counselling possible? *Lancet* 338. pp.998-1001

Clarke, A.J. and Parsons, E.P. (1992), Screening, ethics and the law. Correspondence in *BMJ,* 306. January.pp. 14-29.

Farrant, W. (1985), Who's for amniocentesis? The politics of prenatal screening in Homans H (ed.), *Sexual politics of reproduction* Vermont USA , Gower pp. 272-293.

Glaser, B. and Strauss, A. (1967), *The discovery of grounded theory: strategies For qualitative research.* New York , Aldine

Graham, H. (1984), Surveying through stories, in Bell C. and Roberts H. *Social researching: politics, problems, practice.* London, Routledge. pp.104-124.

Green, J.M. (1994), Women's experience of prenatal screening and diagnosis, in Abramsky L. and Chapple J. (ed.) *Prenatal diagnosis: the human side* London , Chapman and Hall.

Hammersley, M. (1992), *What's wrong with ethnography : methodological explorations.* London , Routledge

Hammersley, M. (1993), *Social research : philosophy, politics and practice*. London, Sage

Hammersley, M. and Atkinson, P. (1995), (2nd Edition) *Ethnography : principles in practice*. London, Routledge

Lofland, J. and Lofland, L.H. (1984), *Analyzing social settings : a guide to qualitative observation and analysis*. Belmont, Wadsworth.

Murcott, A. (1987), Conceptions of food: a sociological analysis'. Unpublished PhD, University of Wales College of Cardiff.

Parsons, E.P. and Atkinson, P.A. (1992), Lay constructions of genetic risk. *Sociology of Health and Illness*. 14 (4) pp. 437-455.

Parsons, E.P. and Atkinson, P.A. (1993), Genetic risk and reproduction. *The Sociological Review*. 41 (3). pp. 679-706.

Parsons, E.P. and Clarke, A.J. (1993), Genetic risk : women's understanding of carrier risks in Duchenne muscular dystrophy. *Journal of Medical Genetics* 30. pp.562-566.

Rothman, B.K. (1987), *The tentative pregnancy : prenatal diagnosis and the future of motherhood* New York, Penguin Books.

Strauss, A.L. (1987), *Qualitative analysis for social scientists*. Cambridge, Cambridge University Press.

Thomas, W.I. (1937), *Primitive behaviour : an introduction to the social sciences* New York, McGraw Hill.

van Maanen, J. (1983), (ed.) *Qualitative methodology*. California, Sage

Wald, N. and Law, M. (1992), Screening, ethics and the law. Correspondence in *BMJ* Vol.305. 10 October 1992, pp.41-63.

Yoxen, E.J. (1982), Constructing genetic disease in Wright P. and Treacher A. (ed.) *The problem of medical knowledge : examining the social construction of medicine*. Edinburgh, Edinburgh University Press.

# 6 In the company of other women: A case study of menopause support groups

*Trish Harding*

> Women and the menopause is as much a study of women and doctors, women and society, and women and the media, as it is of women and what happens to their body when their ovaries retire or are removed.
>
> (Kyle, 1980 p.3)

## Introduction

It will be argued here that the study of women's experience of the menopause should not be confined largely to the realms of medical science. As an enormously complex anthropological and sociological subject area, it demands an interdisciplinary research approach and one which, above all, uses a woman-centred perspective. Whilst studies conducted through clinical trials are informative about the way in which women experience the menopause physically, it is helpful to employ qualitative research methods to gain a more textured and subjective understanding of the menopause; not one simply concerned with the cause, effect and prevalence of symptoms or syndromes.

Unlike other issues associated with women's reproductive health, there have been few attempts within the women's health movement to extend our knowledge of the menopause; to 'demedicalise' it and to place it within the social and cultural context of women's position in society. As Greer (1991, p.18) suggests:

> One of the tasks that needs to be done is that the climacteric needs to be rescued from the fog of prejudice that surrounds it. The menopausal woman is the prisoner of a stereotype

and will not be rescued from it until she has begun to tell her own story.

It is also curious that despite its universality to women, they themselves have remained relatively silent regarding their menopausal experiences. It may be argued, as Greer (1991) does, that this silence can be attributed, at least in part, to a campaign led by men to eliminate the menopause in an attempt to keep women unchanged. However, women's silence may also be the result of ambiguity surrounding the status of the menopause as a rite of passage. While undoubtedly significant to women as a period of transition (indeed the change is marked in varying ways), the menopause is not celebrated (or welcomed) as a rite of passage, unlike other life course events such as the onset of menstruation or the change from single woman to married woman.

This chapter discusses a research study of women's experience of the menopause among attendees of menopause support or self-help health groups in England and Scotland during the late 1980s. The research was carried out for a higher degree The study formed part of an examination of British health education policy and practice more generally. It looked at ways in which women were organising themselves to provide information and support on the menopause in contrast to that available through more conventional models of health education. Moreover it sought to develop a sociological understanding of women's experience of the menopause which could inform the future planning and provision of health education on this topic. The research findings point to the need for an analysis of the menopause as a social event shaped by historical factors and linked to cultural norms and values.

**A sociological understanding of menopause**

The differential experience of the menopause, both physically and emotionally, is not merely due to different biologies but also to women's cultural background and socio-economic position (WHO, 1981). In other words, the menopause is not only a biological event, it is also a social event. One of the most significant factors affecting women's experience of the menopause and the way they feel about themselves is the attitudes of others towards them at this time. Attitudes towards the menopause, and menopausal women, can be located in the wider structural and cultural context of women's role as procreator.

In many Western cultures, prevailing attitudes towards the menopause are negative (Flint, 1975; Greer, 1991). In a society which defines women through their reproductive functions the menopause, as the ending of reproductive life, is overlaid with connotations of loss and hopelessness. It can represent, as Anderson and McPherson point out, '..loss of femininity, a symbolic castration and entry into old age' (1983 p.63). In her exploration of the language of menopause, Reitz noticed that 'most menopausal language implies that the best is over...' (1985 p.16). The use of negative language to label and classify menopausal women not only encourages women to view the menopause as a stigma it also serves as a means of social control. If, for instance, women of menopausal age are justifiably angry or making a complaint about a situation, they are often dismissed, ignored or humoured on the grounds that they are menopausal and therefore going through a 'funny period' (Fairlie *et al*, 1987; Hedges, 1985).

Because of the significance assigned by society to such negative labels and classifications, (that is to say they are generally accepted and shared by other members of society), negative stereotypes of menopausal woman are created. A group member in this study described one such stereotype: 'I do think menopausal women are stereotyped ... a bit of a joke really - past it, overweight, boring, invisible and slightly neurotic ("it's her age you know")'.

Negative stereotypes of this kind are more readily accepted in our society because the experiences of women, and particularly older women, are regarded as less important than those of men (Arber & Ginn, 1991, Sontag, 1978). Within the ideology of reproduction, fertility and femininity are immutably linked (Ussher, 1989). Accordingly, loss of fertility marks the loss of a major part of a woman's femininity - her sexual identity as a potential mother. It may be argued that sexuality cannot be separated from this package. Because motherhood is celebrated in our society, and for some traditionalists child-bearing and child-rearing are considered to be the main contribution of women to society (Miles, 1991), the ability to bear children becomes a necessary part of a woman's sexual attractiveness. This can be placed alongside Weideger's (1978) argument that a woman is sexually desirable to men only as long as her sexuality can inspire fear. Men's fear and awe of women's sexuality is embedded within the cultural myths and taboos surrounding menstruation and the mystical properties of menstrual blood (Birke & Best, 1980; Shuttle & Redgrove, 1986; Weideger, 1978). This theory prescribes that once a woman is no longer menstruating she no longer has the sexual power of a nubile women which gives her the potential to harm men. The menopause, therefore, is not only equated with loss of femininity but also with a loss of sexuality. Within this discourse, women who no longer serve men (both in terms of their fertility and their sexuality) are seen as unnatural and ugly (McDonald & Rich, 1984).

Negative attitudes towards the menopause are also the consequence of its association with ageing. Attitudes towards the menopause mirror the negative attitudes towards old age prevalent in a society that fears death and places a premium on youth and youthfulness (Sontag, 1978; Miles, 1991). However, there is a marked gender differential in the ageism arising from such attitudes. Ageing has a special stigma for women because, in addition, it represents the loss of fertility and sexuality, both of which are venerated in our society. Having lost their youth and their fertility, women can no longer be sexually attractive; sexuality of any kind for older women is culturally taboo, and therefore deviant. In her discussion of the double standard of ageing, Sontag goes as far as suggesting that for many women, ageing represents '..a humiliating process of gradual sexual disqualification' (1978 p.75).

In contrast, men age, yet, as they do not lose their reproductive capacity they are still presented as sexually desirable. Nor are they subjected in the same way as women to negative images of themselves in the mass media; images characterised by derogatory terms such as 'old hag', 'old bag', 'crone'. There is no male equivalent of the stereotypical 'asexual, incompetent, depressed and ridiculous older woman' (Ussher, 1989 p.110). These images are both pervasive and powerful. Older women, therefore, not only experience systematic discrimination through institutionalised sexism and heterosexism, but also through institutionalised ageism.

**Research strategy**

The research reported in this chapter aimed to examine the appropriateness of two contrasting models of health education, the 'conventional' and the 'community development' modes, in relation to women's health information needs concerning the menopause. I decided that an examination of the community development model could take place through a survey of menopause support groups and that the material collected would form a discrete case study. Yin (1984) has suggested that case studies are suited to a situation where 'how' or 'why' questions are being posed, when the researcher has little or no control over events, and when the focus is on a contemporary phenomenon within some real-life context. However, before embracing the case study approach as a research method on this occasion, it was necessary to rehearse the debate concerning its methodological integrity.

Although widely used in social science research, particularly in the area of social anthropology, the validity of the case study as a form of empirical enquiry has been questioned by many researchers. A common criticism is the extent to which the case study, as a single example of a phenomenon, can be used to make scientific generalisations in support of some theoretical analysis. The problem is one of external validity or the typicality of the case which is being used (Clyde Mitchell, 1983). Yin (1984) points out that this problem is not specific to the case study technique and draws parallels with the difficulties of generalising from a single experiment. In his defence of the case study Yin (1984) states that it should not be viewed as a sample. Whilst it cannot, like the experiment, be used for the purposes of statistical inference, it can be used to generalise theoretical propositions. Clyde Mitchell (1983) suggests, too, that inference from a case study is based on the validity of the analysis rather than the representativeness of the events. He argues that the process of extrapolating from any one case study to like situations in general is based on logical rather than statistical inference. The significance of a case study, therefore, lies in its explanatory power rather than its typicality.

It is evident from the debate that the case study may be used as an analytical tool in different ways. It certainly appeared to suit the nature and context of my study - a small scale and largely qualitative examination of a particular model of health education - and its illuminative qualities were a particularly attractive feature. A key component of the research design for a case study is the 'unit(s) of analysis' (Yin, 1984). This refers to the case (an event or entity) to be studied. In this study, the case was to be the activities of menopause support groups.

Among the proliferation of women's groups which have formed themselves in recent years are groups which focus on specific health issues and life events such as the menopause. Although there is not, as yet, a national network of self-help groups for the menopause, many local groups exist to offer support and information to women living in their area. Whilst some see themselves purely as menopause groups, others operate under the title of 'women's health groups' and cover a range of women's health issues. In order to look at the activities of such groups as a form of health education and support to women experiencing the menopause, a number of groups were contacted and asked if they would be prepared to participate in a postal questionnaire survey. Time, cost and access constraints (the groups were dispersed over a wide geographical area), necessitated a postal questionnaire in contrast to telephone or personal interviews. In planning

102

the questionnaire, Foley's study of women's self-help health groups provided a valuable guide to possible question areas (Foley, 1985). The questionnaire was constructed to elicit qualitative data in preference to quantitative, both in order to gain as much information as possible on the 'process' of health education within the groups, and to allow group members to express their own interpretation of its success in meeting their needs. Open-ended and probing questions were used for this purpose. To ensure understanding of the questions, some were repeated later in the questionnaire using a slightly different wording and format. Questions were addressed to the group rather than individual group members. The decision to ask for a collective response rather than several individual responses was felt to be in the spirit of the democratic and collective way in which self-help groups aspire to work.

The survey sought to build a profile of the groups and their activities (including quantitative data on membership characteristics, funding). A key part of the research also sought to develop an understanding of women's experience of the menopause. In order to appreciate the range and diversity of experiences from group members, I decided to enhance the information provided on the questionnaires with requests for individual narratives. As a means of incorporating this biographical data, groups were asked in the covering letter if, in addition to completing the questionnaire, one or two women in each group would be prepared to write in as much detail as they wished a personal account of their particular experience of the menopause. As a guide to writing these accounts, a checklist of suggested areas was enclosed. These encouraged the women to comment on such aspects as the attitudes and stereotypes they may have encountered, what they felt to be most significant about their experiences, why they joined the group and what they felt to be important about the group. By inviting comment on these aspects and thus to a degree pre-structuring the information provided, it was accepted that the responses would not be pure narrative in the sense of women telling their own stories but would offer an individual or personal account to complement the group response represented in the questionnaire.

The process of drawing together a sample for the survey proved lengthy and piecemeal. As Foley (1985) discovered, when doing research within the voluntary sector there is a need to allow for the reality of the workings of voluntary groups and organisations, who, without full-time or paid workers may take some time to respond to requests for information. In attempting to trace the details of groups it was necessary to rely upon a wide variety of sources. Once traced, each group was contacted by telephone, both to ascertain the current status of the groups and to find out whether or not it would be willing to participate in the survey. The final sample comprised

25 groups. All the groups were located in urban areas within England and Scotland. It had not been possible to trace the existence of groups in Wales. Questionnaires were sent out with a letter explaining the aim and purpose of the research and a stamped addressed envelope for completed questionnaires and personal accounts. A period of two months was allowed for the return of questionnaires after which time follow-up letters were sent to those groups who had not responded.

A total of 15 completed questionnaires were received, a response rate of 60%. The questionnaires were accompanied by 7 personal accounts received from individual group members. These took the form of letters and written statements all of which were rich and illuminating, and occasionally very moving, in their content. Some respondents, for instance, referred to changes in family circumstances and the impact of these on their experience of the menopause:

> I have not attended my GP for 'menopausal' problems and feel I am almost through this stage with very few physical upsets. The emotional strains, especially three years of coping with my mother, were quite considerable but the group was invaluable for letting off steam. ..... Being a member of this particular group has meant that I have met many women who were complete strangers and with whom I now have a deep personal attachment. It has given me a greater understanding of the strength and adaptability of women to all sorts of pressures. It has helped me to set my own life in perspective and to consider myself as a worthy person.
>
> (Personal Account: Group A)

The survey provided a wealth of information on the nature of menopause groups. Analysis of the completed questionnaires was carried out in two stages. Firstly, question responses were extracted, collated and recorded in a summarised form. Secondly, the information was grouped into categories which would enable examination of the key research questions. Categories included: the origins and history of each group; their aims; their activities; their contact with other groups and organisations; their views on other forms of help or support; their funding and resources; their organisation and structure; their membership profile; the problems they had encountered. With the data organised in this way, it was possible to draw out the broad characteristics of a 'typical group' and to identify any interesting deviations to the typical. Information contained in the personal accounts was similarly grouped into categories. These broadly followed the checklist provided of suggested areas for comment. These categories offered additional information about women's experience of the menopause and their participation in the group. For example, now experience of the menopause matched individual expectations. What was important about the group and how it has helped. Where relevant, extracts from the personal accounts were incorporated into the analysis of questionnaire responses to support findings.

Decisions regarding the research design and methods were not only governed by its status as a higher degree project (see also Jones' chapter in this volume) but also by a commitment to what has been variously defined as 'feminist research' (McRobbie, 1982; Roberts, 1981; Stanley & Wise, 1983 & 1993). The concept of feminist research has arisen in response to a feminist critique of theory and practice in the social sciences. In relation to sociology, for example, Oakley (1983) has demonstrated the sexist bias within much social science work towards research concerned with the interests and activities of men; a tendency which serves to omit or distort the experience of women. In their critique of malestream sociology, Abbott and Wallace (1990 p.1) echo this point: 'There is still a tendency to generalize from male samples to the whole population, and textbooks 'add women on' as an appendix - an extra topic or chapter -rather than incorporating research findings on women'. A further key theme in the feminist critique concerns the need for a non-sexist methodology. Attention is drawn to the gender dimensions of particular research methods and the use of terminology such as 'masculine' and 'hard' in relation to quantitative methods and data; and 'feminine' and 'soft' in relation to qualitative methods and data.

For writers such as Stanley and Wise (1983 and 1993) and Harding (1987), however, feminist research has to be constructed out of contemporary feminist theory and not merely be concerned to remove sexist biases or the inferred sexism implicit in distinctions between quantitative and qualitative methods. It therefore has to be reflexive and has to take account of the researcher's own feminist consciousness and her experience of being a woman. This necessarily involves an understanding of women's position as that of an oppressed social group (Oakley, 1990). Clegg (1985) has also argued against the formulation of a specific 'feminist methodology' as some coherent, unified set of practices and principles. She cites the argument put forward by Kelly (1978) that feminist research is feminist not in terms of the peculiarity of its methods, but in terms of the questions it starts with and the interpretation placed on the results. In this sense, the research relationship should not be oppressive or patronising; and the knowledge produced should be accessible to the researched, and to other women. The presentation and language of research findings is therefore important.

Graham (1984) has stressed the need to design research methods which are sensitive to the structure of women's lives. Her exploration of narratives is useful in this respect. She argues that narratives provide a way in which women can be involved in studies of their lives yet not be oppressed by these studies. Narratives can temper the presence of exploitation and misrepresentation in survey research that concerns the experiences of women. They offer a situation whereby women can participate as subjects on their own terms. Through 'telling their own story' women are not confined or constrained by the structure imposed by the researcher and can be more involved in the presentation and interpretation of the knowledge they are contributing (Graham, 1984; Stanley & Wise, 1993). The format is self-structured. Narratives not only enable women to mark the boundaries of their contribution but also provide the interpretative framework through which it will be constructed. Furthermore, narratives provide a vehicle through which women can communicate the complexity of their lives. They shed light on the shadowy areas of women's social world not usually captured within the language of questionnaires and interviews.

## Research findings

The data collected using the survey suggests that the support groups played a key social function in enabling women to share together their knowledge and information, whilst at the same time providing support and friendship:

> Friends have been made at the group that I would be sorry not to see again. When we speak openly at these meetings about our bodies there is bound to be a bond between us all which you do not get in everyday conversations with friends and acquaintances.
>
> (Personal Account, Group H)

The benefit of being able to talk with others who are going through a similar experience was strongly emphasised in the questionnaires and personal accounts. As one respondent remarked; 'We all agree it's having someone to talk to who doesn't poo poo what you say that helps the most'. Comments from another group also illustrate this point:

> We found the best therapy was to talk to others and realise from discussion that you're not the only one with problems and that given time, the symptoms do go away. A lot of women coming along to the group did benefit from talking out their problems, perhaps because it was informal and they were not embarrassed, showing their feelings and at times having a little weep.
>
> (Questionnaire, Group M)

Many women placed an emphasis on emotional or psychological problems and the part these play in women's menopausal experience. Often these appeared to be a consequence of their anxiety over what was happening to them physically. An understanding of the way women experience the menopause cannot simply rest on an understanding of the frequency and intensity of 'symptoms' but also on the meaning women themselves assign to these. In their research, Fairhurst and Lightup (1981) found that although women may use the literature to map out what can reasonably be expected during the menopause (ie the normal course of events), for one group of women, interpretation of this knowledge was heavily influenced by what they perceived as being 'normal' for themselves. Thus, in this case, the absence or presence of certain 'classic symptoms' may only be problematic if it does not conform to a woman's self-assessment of her individual normality.

The groups in my study indicated that, through discussion women were able to feel less isolated in the negative attitudes they were experiencing. For many women, the group gave them space to think about such attitudes and the problems arising from these, and to formulate possible solutions; in contrast individually the process of simply defining the problem could be difficult. One group member commented in her personal account:

> I think menopausal women are stereotyped, we are nothing but a music hall joke in many cases. One doctor who came to speak to the group openly admitted that hardly any mention at all during their training as doctors is given to the menopause. Hopefully, with our generation and possibly more so with our daughters, we will no longer sit back and put up with being fobbed off.
>
> (Personal Account, Group H)

By making women more aware of the social and cultural context in which they were experiencing their problems, the groups were also providing a powerful tool with which women could challenge misconception and myth surrounding the menopause. Misconception and myth can flourish where there is a lack of appropriate and accessible health education. When discussing the health promotion materials available to them, the groups highlighted a desire for more comprehensive and less patronising information which recognises the diversity in women's experience of the menopause and is more appropriate to their lives. By coming together in a group, women were able to discuss issues not normally addressed within existing information but which they themselves defined as important, (for example relationships between women and their doctors). This process can be empowering because it validates women's own experiences. Women in the groups reported feeling more confident and assertive in their use of health services and feeling stronger in dealing with the negative attitudes of others. For example:

> Attitudes vary, in general women GPs tend to be more sympathetic (unless they are postmenopausal). Older male GPs tend to offer tranquillisers, and are against HRT (Hormone Replacement Therapy), younger GPs tend to offer HRT. Many male GPs are dismissive. Women are nervous and communication can be very difficult. After coming to the group some women have actually changed their GP.
>
> (Questionnaire, Group E)

In addition to offering practical support and learning (and being a form of health education dissemination in themselves), groups appeared to be making a substantial contribution to the limited pool of multi-media information on the menopause. Four of the groups had produced their own materials, some of which had been printed and were available for purchase (leaflets, a video and cassette tape). One group had taken part in a television and a radio programme. The materials were based on their own experiences of the menopause and on what they felt other women wanted to know. In this way the women were demystifying medical knowledge and extending their own knowledge to other women.

The comfort and reassurance available through the collective effort of talking with other women in a group situation is particularly effective where women are 'off schedule' and do not have friends who are also menopausal (Nelson, 1984). The emotional support offered by a group was also useful in situations where women found their doctors unsympathetic or too busy to provide such a counselling role, or where women found their family unable to understand the problems they were experiencing.

> I know I am lucky to have a supportive and loving family, but there is a limit to the amount I would discuss with them about the menopause as basically they can't understand the problems never having experienced them. All the members of the group can understand and we discuss everything freely and honestly without coffee morning politeness. .... I certainly feel that I can talk openly without the fear of boring the members and I can think of nowhere else I could get the same support at this particular time of my life.
>
> (Personal Account, Group B)

Support from families appeared variable. In some cases there was little significant exchange of information or support among women in the family; a situation which Hedges (1985) also found in her study of women and the menopause. Similarly, support from local health services appeared lacking. The view of the vast majority of groups was the NHS does not adequately serve the needs of women. Groups commented on the insufficient funding and provision for women's health concerns, particularly those of middle-aged women. They were critical of the lack of research into the menopause, the lack of well-woman centres, menopause clinics and counselling or emotional support, and the poor availability of smear tests and other regular checks.

The advantages and benefits of menopause support groups highlighted by the case study match, in many respects, those discussed in the literature on self-help groups. However, there would also seem to be problems associated with menopause groups which limit their suitability for all women. Women interviewed in other studies on the menopause have, for instance, expressed an ambivalence and reticence towards such groups which may be due to the stigma and taboos still attached to the menopause and an unwillingness by women to openly label themselves as menopausal (Fairlie, 1984). A further factor which may deter women from joining a group is the common perception that self-help groups are a middle-class activity. Whilst the social class analysis of groups in this case study revealed a social class distribution of members close to the national average and not favourably weighted towards a middle-class membership, it was nevertheless necessary for women to have no or few material constraints on their participation.

## Conclusion

The case study described in this chapter aimed to present qualitative data on women's experience of the menopause. Rather than focus simply on women's experience of physical and psychological symptoms, the survey of menopause support groups sought to illuminate social aspects of the menopause, such as negative labelling and stereotyping, and sought to reveal the social role performed by groups in helping women to deal with these aspects.

The research indicates the need to construct a social model of the menopause which places women's experience of this event within the context of their entire lives, and in particular within the context of ageing and the ideology of reproduction. Such a model would attempt to retrieve our understanding of the menopause from the medical community by demedicalising it and reconstructing it on women's own terms. It would build on the feminist critique of health whereby feminists have attempted to discover how far patterns of female ill-health can be explained by the nature of women's lives and by the social construction of the female role. In other words, women's health cannot be viewed within a social and cultural vacuum. Within this discourse, research on women's health must entail a recognition of the effect on health of the powerlessness and feelings of alienation which women, and older women especially, experience. In the context of the menopause, many writers refer to changes or crises within a woman's domestic, social or work life which can make the menopause a vulnerable period (Fairlie *et al*, 1987). Hence, in addition to the effect of factors such as institutionalised ageism and sexism, they point to the possible relevance of such factors as an increased responsibility for ageing relatives or the loss of a partner which may be coupled with a feeling of economic insecurity. One of the groups in this study expressed a view of the menopause as; 'A very difficult time of life all round - teenage children - menopausal husbands - elderly parents - career problems etc'. We need to appreciate, however, that the significance of these factors will depend upon the expectations women have about themselves and their role in the family and/or at work. A social model of the menopause also acknowledges the significance of the social aspects of the menopause in the ways in which women experience it physically. Women may find the negative attitudes towards the menopause, ageing, and older women, very stressful. Stress of this nature may then compound the physical conditions and give rise to, or increase depression.

The menopause has become increasingly medicalised in recent years and certainly the growing debate over the use of hormone replacement therapy has placed it more prominently on the public agenda. Within this scenario it is essential that a non-medical perspective of the menopause is made equally available. A social model of the menopause stresses the importance of understanding the social, political, economic and cultural forces which affect women's opportunities for health and wellbeing. Qualitative research plays a crucial role in developing such an understanding. It also offers a process through which women can become better informed and better able to deal with major life events such as the menopause.

The research study reported here has used qualitative methods to enable a wide range of menopause groups and their members to tell of their experiences. The decision to direct the questionnaire to the group as opposed to individuals within the group was a special feature of the research. While this may well have proved an interesting exercise for the groups, it did result in a tendency to generalise about their experiences. The use of a postal questionnaire, accompanied by narratives, facilitated access to a larger number of women (on average groups had 10-12 members) than would have been feasible through interviews. For the purposes of this case study, it was not necessary to visit the groups in order to follow up questionnaire responses with personal interviews or to employ observational techniques. Undoubtedly, there is a place for the triangulation of data in this way and further research on health education for the menopause would benefit from the use of qualitative methods which can provide indepth accounts of women's experiences.

**References**

Abbott P. and Wallace C. (1990), *An introduction to sociology: feminist perspectives*, London, Routledge.

Anderson A. and McPherson A. (eds) (1983), *Women's problems in general practice*, Oxford, Oxford University Press, Series 4

Arber S. and Ginn J. (1991), *Gender and later life: a sociological analysis of resources and constraints*, London, Sage.

Birke L. and Best S. (1980), The tyrannical womb: menstruation and menopause, in The Brighton Women and Science Group (eds), *Alice through the microscope*, London, Virago, pp. 89-107.

Clegg S. (1985), Feminist methodology - fact or fiction?, *Quality and Quantity*, 19 (1) pp.83-97

Clyde Mitchell J. (1983), Case and situation analysis, *The Sociological Review*, 31 (2) pp.187-211

Fairhurst E. and Lightup R. (1981), *The notion of normality and the interpretation of physiological events: the case of the menopause*, unpublished paper presented to the Third International Congress on the Menopause, 9-12 June 1981, Ostend, Belgium

Fairlie J. A. (1984), *The Menopause: A study of available information sources and the extent to which women use them*, unpublished M.Sc dissertation, Centre for Science Education, University of London

Fairlie J., Nelson J. and Popplestone R. (1987*), Menopause: a time for positive change*, Poole, Blandford Press.

Flint M. (1975), The menopause: reward or punishment?, *Psychosomatics*, 16 ( 4) pp.161-163

Foley R. (1985), *Women and health care: self-help health groups in Britain*, Manchester, Equal Opportunities Commission.

Graham H. (1984), Surveying through stories, in Bell C. and Roberts H. (eds), *Social research, politics, problems and practice*, London, Routledge & Kegan Paul, pp.104-124.

Greer G. (1991), *The change: women, ageing and the menopause*, London, Hamish Hamilton,

Harding S. (1987), (ed.), *Feminism and methodology*, Bloomington and Milton Keynes, Indiana University Press and Open University Press.

Hedges L. A. (1985), *Women and the menopause*, unpublished dissertation, Diploma in Health Education, University of Leeds

Kelly A. (1978), Feminism and research, *Women's Studies International Quarterly*, 1 pp. 225-232

Kyle D. (1980), *Women and medicine*, Manchester, EOC/PLC.

MacDonald B. and Rich Cc (1984), *Look me in the eye*, London, Women's Press,

McRobbie A. (1982), The politics of feminist research: between talk, text and action, *Feminist Review*, 12 pp.47-57

Miles A. (1991), *Women, health and medicine*, Milton Keynes, Open University Press,

Nelson J. (1983), *Women and ageing*, Unpublished MA Dissertation in Women's Studies, University of Kent

Oakley A. (1983), Women and health policy, in Lewis J (ed.), *Women's welfare, women's rights*, London, Croom Helm, pp.103-129.

Oakley A. (1990), Who's afraid of the randomized controlled trial?, in Roberts H (ed.), *Women's health counts*, London, Routledge, pp.167-194.

Reitz R. (1985), *Menopause: a positive approach*, London, Allen & Unwin.

Roberts H. (1981), *Doing feminist research*, London, Routledge & Kegan Paul.

Shuttle P. and Redgrove P. (1986), *The wise wound: menstruation and everywoman*, London, Paladin Grafton Books.

Sontag S. (1978), The double standard of ageing, in Carver V. and Liddiard P. (eds), *An ageing population*, Sevenoaks, Hodder and Stoughton in association with The Open University Press, pp.72-80

Stanley L. and Wise S. (1983), *Breaking out: feminist consciousness and feminist research*, London, Routledge and Kegan Paul.

Stanley L. and Wise S. (1993), *Breaking out again: feminist ontology and epistemology*, London, Routledge.

Ussher J. (1989), *The psychology of the female body*, London, Routledge and Kegan Paul,

Weideger P. (1978), *Female cycles*, London, Women's Press.

WHO (1981), *Research on the menopause*, report of a Scientific Group, Technical Report Series 670, Geneva

Yin R. K. (1984), Case study research design and methods, *Applied Social Research Methods* Series Volume 5, California, Sage Publications.

# 7 Focus groups, young people and sex education

*Lesley Pugsley*

## Introduction

> 'I say, I say, I say, - how could MI5 avoid security leaks?'
> 'I don't know? How could MI5 avoid security leaks?'
> 'It could recruit teenagers as agents:- They never give *anything* away!'

While it is not particularly funny, many parents and teachers of adolescents will appreciate, and to varying degrees share, the sentiments expressed in the above joke. Most will have experienced at first hand, the facility which young people have of communicating with adults on a strictly 'need to know' basis. The idea of getting teenagers to *talk* to a researcher about *sex* and to offer opinions on the ways in which it is taught in school, and about the perceived gaps in their knowledge and their needs, might seem a somewhat foolhardy, if not impossible task. However, this is what I aimed to do (Pugsley, 1995). This chapter sets out to highlight how focus group interviews can operate as a means of researching such a sensitive topic area as sex education with young people. It looks at data generated from such an approach, and aims to highlight the significance of both gender and academic route in the dynamic of group interaction.

## The 'right' way to do it: sex education and policy

Sex education is currently one of the most controversial and politicised aspects of the school curriculum. In 1986 Her Majesties Inspectorate of Schools (HMI), acknowledged that sexual relationships are an integral part of all our lives and so recognised the role which sex education plays in a child's education, and the transition to adulthood. The Children Act (1989) also recognised sexuality as a potent force affecting adolescents. However, it can be argued that the debates about sex education are concerned more with issues of ideological purity than any desire to offer young people a comprehensive programme of teaching.

During the late 1970s and early 1980s attempts were made, in some local authority areas in the United Kingdom, to accommodate differences in sexual orientation, gender and ethnicity through educational initiatives (Thomson, 1994; Chitty, 1994). Increasingly efforts were made to develop a partnership between the disparate health and education philosophies, so that a more holistic approach to sex education could be adopted. However, for the influential New Right of the Conservative Party, any suggestion of a liberal sex education curriculum, particularly one which could be seen to be raising awareness of issues relating to teenage sexuality or sexual diversity, was clearly abhorrent. In consequence there was a strong political backlash which came in the form of demands to end what was seen as a *laissez faire* approach to personal and social education (Thomson, 1994).

These demands led to the installation of a series of political initiatives which were formulated to validate traditional, heterosexual family structures and values, reflecting them through the education system. These initiatives have served to reject the realities of the pluralist society which young people are experiencing in their daily lives. Within the sex education curriculum, they have been translated into the reinforcement of stereotypical gender roles. Examples of this can be found in the 1986 Education (No.2) Act, which located sex education within a legal framework. Responsibility for the formulation of sex education policies was removed from local education authorities (LEAs), and placed within the remit of individual schools and their boards of governors. Section 18, Clause 2, of the Act allowed the governors discretionary powers over whether sex education should be taught and if it were, what materials the curriculum should contain. Both moralising and moralistic overtones were clear in Clause 46 of the 1986 Act, which required that, if sex education was provided in a school, 'it should be taught with due regard to moral considerations, and the values of family life'.

The 1988 Education Reform Act restated the role of school governing bodies, but attempted to curb their discretionary powers by indicating that all pupils were to be taught those aspects of sex education which comprised parts of the National Curriculum science syllabus. The now infamous Clause 28 of the Local Government Act 1989, made it illegal for local authorities to 'intentionally promote homosexuality'. Although this did not specifically prevent schools from giving pupils information about homosexuality as part of a sex education programme, it did serve to compound the general climate of uncertainty which surrounds the teaching of the topic. Scott (1994) suggests that the feeling of paranoia which existed among those associated with sex education in schools served to undermine any attempts at providing a holistic approach to the subject.

Over the past decade, the Government's approach to sex education has been in line with the majority of it's other policies for education, demonstrating what Bash and Coulby (1991) refer to as contradiction and conflict. The Departments of Health and Education have once again been set at odds. Health educators have taken the view that providing teenagers with information on contraceptives and sexually transmitted diseases (including AIDS/HIV) is a means of achieving the targets identified in the *Health of the Nation* White Paper (1992). In contrast, the Department of Education offers schools, parents and pupils confused messages about sex education, compartmentalising information into subject categories and prescribing their curriculum content. The 1993 Education Act is the culmination of competing strands of political ideology inherent in both *Thatcherism* and *Majorism*. Within the 1993 Act, the government's exposed liberalism of 'choice' rivals its authoritarian populism, and prescribes sexuality and sexual relationships within the confines of a stable family unit. In consequence, the reinforcement of traditional concepts of gender and sexuality (which underpin the sex education curriculum), serve as a means of social control, since sex education programmes do not address the reality of sexual diversity. Rather they are based on the assumption that 'young people are, and will remain, heterosexual' (Fine, 1988 p.92).

While being both a controversial and politicised aspect of the school curriculum, (which effectively replicates dominant cultural forms of gender relations and sexuality), the sex education young people receive is a relatively under-researched area. A few studies have adopted a quantitative focus (for example, Farrell, 1978; Allen, 1987) in order to measure the efficacy of various teaching programmes. More recently there has been some qualitative research conducted (Wolpe, 1988; Measor, 1989; Mac an Ghaill, 1991). These studies have focused on issues within the classroom. They have been particularly concerned with pupil behaviour, patterns of resistance and the moral order of the schools themselves. In contrast, this chapter concentrates on the opinions of young people and focuses on what it is they have to say, both about the sex education which they have received and their attitudes to issues relating to teenage sexuality.

I had previously researched sex education and pupil perceptions, using a self complete questionnaire approach (Pugsley, 1994). In this study, 202 students in year 12, (Lower Sixth), from three schools in one county in South Wales were surveyed. The aim of this research had been to determine the approaches to the teaching of sex education and the levels of pupil satisfaction with the programmes offered, based on the religious affiliation of different schools (Roman Catholic, Anglican, and Local Authority controlled). Although no significant differences emerged from the pupils in respect of the religious contexts of the schools, there were considerable differences in the responses, related to the gender of the respondents. Clearly, while a questionnaire survey is useful in order to identify statistical trends, such a quantitative approach does not 'give voice' to the divergent opinions of those researched. Therefore in an attempt to allow the teenagers the opportunity to express their opinions on this topic, and to further investigate the gendered differences which had been noted, a qualitative approach was adopted (Pugsley, 1995).

This chapter sets out to demonstrate the ways in which focus groups can be used as a method of qualitative research. It describes their use when applied to researching sensitive subjects. The advantages and disadvantages of focus group research are discussed. Reliance on groups who are known to one another, can allow for lively debate with members challenging the opinions and comments of others. However as this chapter shows, some of those pupils engaged in the discussions may have had 'guilty knowledge' of the sexual history of other members of the group and this may have served to prescribe and delimit the range of debate.

**Entering the arena: focus groups as method**

Kitzinger (1994, p.159) defines focus groups as 'group discussions organised to explore a specific set of issues'. Their use has been the subject of considerable controversy and criticism over time. It has been suggested that focus groups fail to provide hard data and that the opinions expressed may not be representative of a larger population, (because of their size and the idiosyncratic nature of a group discussion). While Stewart and Shamdasani, (1990, p.15) suggest that 'focus groups can be useful at virtually any point in a research programme', they are frequently used as a means of supplementing and triangulating information collected from quantitative methods. However, there is no *a priori* reason to assume that they need validation. Rather there is a need to acknowledge their full potential as a self contained means of data collection and as a shared component for social research. While they can be useful in exploring sensitive topics, there are both advantages and disadvantages associated with this method. Clearly they are cost effective in terms of researcher time, since a number of informants can be interviewed at one time, and the

117

analysis time is also reduced as there are fewer transcripts (Morgan 1988). However, focus groups rely heavily on the group dynamic for success, since the constituent members discussions of their own experiences and opinions serve to provide the fundamental data (Morgan, 1988; Fielding, 1993).

Focus groups are guided discussions between people ranging from four to twelve in number, six to eight being the optimum number. They combine a laboratory type setting with a less structured format than the controlled experiment which attempts to simulate every day discussion. Rather the groups are *focused* in the sense that they involve some kind of collective activity, such as viewing a film, examining a single health education message or simply debating a particular set of questions. The primary advantage associated with the use of focus groups as a method is that they provide the researcher with access to forms of data that are not readily available using individual interviews or participant observation.

This particular method allowed me to have access to a set of discussions between young people about sexuality and sexual knowledge, which might otherwise have been difficult, if not impossible to obtain. I am a middle aged woman, and I could not have expected to 'hang out' with groups of teenagers as a participant observer and be privy to their conversations about sex. Also, given the sensitivity of the topic, a 'one to one' interview might not have provided much in the way of useful data. Although some authors (Morgan, 1988; Kreuger, 1988; ) suggest that it is best to recruit people who are unknown to each other, I needed to have groups with a shared experience, and both Kitzinger (1994) and Denscombe (1995) offer exemplars of work successfully conducted using this method. Furthermore, sex may be regarded as a topic which is most openly discussed in the company of friends.

The use of a moderator was an issue which required some careful deliberation. Some authors (for example Kreuger, 1988; Morgan, 1988) suggest that special moderator skills are required in order to facilitate the direction of the discussion in focus group research. However it can be argued that the already 'artificial' nature of the group discussion might be further inhibited by the presence of a stranger. Stewart and Shamdasani (1990, p.35) assert that having a designated leader, or moderator, serves to 'eliminate much of the distraction associated with the group developing its own pattern of leadership'. I had decided that an additional presence might be both welcome and necessary. I chose to co-opt a colleague into my research . I felt that I needed to select someone who would be able to interact with young people and feel 'comfortable' during discussions about sex and sexuality. In consequence, I chose a female postgraduate (Kate),

118

who in her mid twenties, fell into an age category between myself and that of the research subjects.

The focus group interviews were conducted at Taff Vale School, which has a sixth form offering courses leading to both the academic A level examinations and the National Vocational Qualifications (NVQ). A total of four focus group interviews were held. Each lasted approximately one hour and the groups were differentiated by gender and academic route being pursued. The discussions took place during the period timetabled for PSE (Personal and Social Education) and the students sat around tables which I had pre-arranged to form a square. The hour long conversations were recorded, with the students knowledge and permission. The recordings were then transcribed. In so doing, I avoided the temptation to clean or tidy the data (Kitzinger, 1994) and the subsequent accounts are reported verbatim. I also took notes in longhand, partly as a precaution against mechanical failure, but also because it provided me with an opportunity to observe the group discretely as I wrote. These notes were to prove vital during the transcribing process, since they allowed me to identify individuals and so differentiate between speakers, especially when there were several voices speaking at once.

In order that there should be some degree of comparison between groups and also to ensure that they remained focused on the topic, I compiled a set of generic questions relating to general topic areas which I hoped to be able to cover in the interviews and arranged them in a loose running order. Under each, I included a few key words which could be used as prompts, should the respondents fail to understand the general line of the questions or should the conversation simply 'dry up'.

When negotiating access to the pupils, I had made it clear to the gatekeeper (Hammersley and Atkinson, 1995) - Mrs Pigeon (Head of Religious Studies at Taff Vale School) - that the successful focus group consisted of between six to eight members. During our meeting, Mrs Pigeon had been quite agreeable to my taking this number of volunteers from the various classes and interviewing them, while she kept the remainder of the group for the normal class teaching session. However, when it came to the actual interviews, I had no control over the number of students in any of the groups. For each of the four sessions, it was made implicit that I was to act as 'supply cover' for the period. I was simply left with the whole class, irrespective of the number of pupils in the group and without predetermining if there were any students who were unwilling to participate in the research. Although none of the students actually elected to leave the room during the interviews, several of them clearly indicated by their general attitude and body language their unwillingness to engage in the discussions and remained 'apart' from the group discussions.

Mrs Pigeon had told me that the student numbers might vary as the PSE lessons, 'are often seen as an opportunity for students, particularly the NVQ groups to bunk off [absent themselves from] school'. In consequence the composition of the groups researched was not uniform in number, and in some cases far from ideal. They eventually comprised of; an 'A' level group of 13 boys; an 'A' level group of 9 girls; an NVQ group of 3 boys and an NVQ group of 13 girls.

The A level boys arrived punctually and were smartly presented, the dress code clearly adhered to. Although the school has no specific uniform for its sixth form students, it does have a code of dress. Jeans are not permitted and students are asked to wear plain navy, black or grey trousers or skirts and primary colour shirts or blouses with sweat shirts or cardigans. They had been told in advance that someone from the university was going to ask them about sex education and they were all prepared to join in the discussion, speaking quite freely among themselves and to both Kate and myself. The A level girls were also on time and clearly 'uniformly' dressed in accordance with the school code. They too were eager to debate topics within the group and were prepared to engage in debate about the various issues discussed.

In contrast to these groups, the interview with the boys studying the NVQ course was almost a non starter. Only one boy, Stevo, arrived on time and his presence prompted Mrs Pigeon to remark that clearly the idea of talking about sex was responsible for his attending, since they hardly ever saw him in school these days. When I told Stevo that, while I was very interested in what he had to say, it would hardly constitute a focus group, he immediately said he would see if he could, 'nab some of the others for you miss 'cos I knows where they skives off to[sic]'. After about ten minutes, he returned accompanied by two more young men from his class, providing me with a smaller than ideal number, but a focus group none the less. All three were rather more casually dressed than the A level groups, and they displayed a tendency to favour sports clothing, T shirts, training tops and jogging pants. However they were very good natured and willingly agreed to participate in the research.

The girls in the NVQ group were very different from the A level girls and quite distinct in their self presentation. They came into the lesson in a leisurely way, the last two girls arriving some ten minutes after the first. Many of the group had long hair which was often coloured and permed into a curly mass (which they wore in an assortment of elaborate styles). A number of them had long fringes which they played with constantly, twisting it through their fingers as the session progressed. Almost all of the group wore make up, which is not permitted by the dress code. Some of the girls wore dark eye liner and mascara, had coloured nails and either very pale, almost white, or very dark plum coloured lips. Their dress was uniform in its similarity, but showed no regard for the plain sober colours required by the school code. They were clearly intent on making a variety of fashion statements, wearing earrings, bracelets and rings, short tight skirts or trousers and fashion tops. This group were clearly ill at ease in the situation, giving the impression that they were uncomfortable with the notion of talking to each other about sex education and especially, perhaps, with us.

In order to introduce both myself and the moderator to the groups, I told the pupils a little about ourselves and our educational backgrounds. I then broached the topic by telling them that the purpose of my research was to find out what they, as consumers of education, thought of the sex education they were receiving. I stressed that by taking the opportunity to talk to me they would enable me to give voice to their opinions. The week before, I began the interviews, Will Carling, (the Captain of the England Rugby Union Team) had been widely reported in the popular press for making unfavourable comments about the English selectors [he had called them a bunch of boring old farts]. This anecdote was topical and served as a good 'ice breaker'. It also allowed me to draw an analogy between the rugby selectors *and* the government, both of whom are remote, autonomous bodies, who make decisions which may be ill-informed, but which none the less impact on a great many others.

**Talking about sex**

Although I had learned from Mrs Pigeon about the ways in which sex education was presented to the various year groups throughout the school, the initial response to the question, 'Tell us about your sex education', was the same from all the groups. They denied that they had received any.

> Sharon:      What's sex education! [laughter from the group].
> Marie:       We don't do that.
> > (Female NVQ group)

> Stevo:       We haven't had a lot.
> > (Male NVQ group)

> Lisa:        Did we do some in form 3?

Rhiannon:      Yes but that was on plants [laughter from the group].

(Female A level group)

With some prompting from Kate (the moderator), the pupils gradually began to recount some of their experiences and feelings about sex education.

Mark:      Videos, things like that really ... most teachers try to cop out of teaching it [sex education]. They put on videos and leave you to it.

Richard:      They mostly show the video and say nothing

Robert :      If they do [talk] its just Biology.

(Male A level group)

Sophie:      We saw a video on *Turtles* once [she laughs and shrugs her shoulders].

(Female A level group)

Sarah:      We did 'ave videos but it was really uh ... I dunno.

Pam:      Oh yeah the Biology video- nothing of any use in *that* was there!

(Female NVQ group)

Each of the groups agreed that teachers are embarrassed and uncomfortable when confronted with a sex education lesson. They were unanimous that with the exception of Mrs Pigeon, all the staff who tried to teach it were useless.

James:      Mrs Pigeon is really up front about everything, and she's fun when she teaches it, she doesn't try to cover anything up.

Robert :      She [Mrs Pigeon] doesn't care ... she just comes straight out with it [boys nod and murmur in agreement].

| James: | Because she doesn't feel embarrassed you sort of keep respect for her. |
|---|---|
| | (Male A level group) |

| Penny: | Mrs P is good, she tells you it straight |
|---|---|
| | (Female A level group) |

| Stevo: | I hate *all* teachers, I can't stand them - there's only two I like, one's Mrs Pigeon. Well all the rest, they just gave me so much trouble when I was in rest of the school, I wouldn't want to hear it [sex education] from a teacher. |
|---|---|
| | (Male NVQ group) |

Most of the students felt that the sex education which they had received at Taff Vale had been a 'waste of time'.

| Mark: | I bunked off most lessons of PSE in the lower school. You did nothing. |
|---|---|
| | (Male A level group) |

| Carolyn: | Most people don't pay attention anyway in PSE, it's boring! |
|---|---|
| | (Female NVQ group) |

Asked where they did get their sex education from, most said that parents feel too embarrassed to approach the subject of sex, and in the main that they had received little formal sex education. Where they had, it had mainly come from older siblings, or from media sources. In the main, boys relied on their friends and the general 'sex chat' of the school yard and the street corner. In the group members accounts, access to information about sex was gendered.

| Sion: | Yeah we get it mostly from our friends. |
|---|---|
| | (Male NVQ group) |

| Gary: | We, well boys generally I suppose, just sort of get the information from each other, and.... |
|---|---|

| Michael: | Channel 4 [Big laugh from the group]. |
|---|---|

| | |
|---|---|
| Robert: | Boys just chat among their mates like... |
| James: | Girls have got their magazines haven't they. I mean there's loads in them about sex and stuff. Well I read my sisters magazines, like *Just Seventeen* [laughter from the group] all right I know ... but I think girls find out more about things from magazines. |

(Male A level group)

The girls confirmed James opinion - they all agreed that they read magazines such as *Just Seventeen* and most particularly *More* which is a fortnightly publication which mixes beauty hints, fashion, pop star gossip and sex. Teenage girls rely heavily on the information it supplies for their sex education.

| | |
|---|---|
| Naomi: | It's *Just Seventeen* when you're little - fourteen to fifteen say *(*group nod and indicate they agree). Now it's *More* |

(Female A level group)

| | |
|---|---|
| Mandy: | We get stuff from magazines and friends, but mainly magazines. |

(Female NVQ group)

When asked who they would turn to if they had a problem or a specific question about sex which needed to be answered, some of the girls said they would ask parents, usually the mother. However they felt that both they and she would be embarrassed. Some of the girls in the NVQ group said they would definitely not want to discuss things with their mothers because they wouldn't want her knowing what they were up to. In the main all the groups felt that they would look to their peers for advice. Kate then asked if this seemed a sensible or reliable source of information.

| | |
|---|---|
| Rhiannon: | I would rather read it in a magazine because then you don't feel so stupid about saying you don't know something. |
| | |
| Naomi: | Depends on your friends - like I know with my friends, some of them are going out with boys and so they know stuff. |

(Female A level group)

Mark: I mean people take it for granted and they say 'oh well it's bound to be right because my mate said ...', well you just accept things, especially when you're younger.

(Male A level group)

These responses suggest that, even though it is viewed as an important source of information, young people do not uncritically accept the advice of their peer group. Advice was regarded as much more reliable if based on experience, as suggested by Naomi. Anxiety about being seen as naive seems to lead these young people to be cautious about seeking advice from such sources, as suggested by Rhiannon, or about accepting any advice given at face value, as suggested by Mark.

Members of all the focus groups felt that they wanted sex education updated and taught by outside agencies in conjunction with PSE in school. In contrast to the questionnaire survey which showed that pupils were largely in favour of mixed groups for sex education (Pugsley, 1994), those interviewed within the focus groups felt that the lessons would benefit from being held in small, single sex groups. This would allow for a freer discussion and would limit embarrassment and showing off (see also Winn, Roker and Coleman, 1995).

The focus group interviews with the sixth form students gave insight into the range of attitudes to the provision of sex education and the various alternative sources of information which young people use in their quests for sex education and advice. The pedagogic styles of presentation are evidently failing, since the students initially denied having received any sex education at the school. I knew this to be incorrect as I had been shown the sex education curriculum taught at Taff Vale by Mrs Pigeon. This suggests that topics need to be introduced specifically and points 'flagged', in order to allow pupils to recognise, and so compartmentalise, that they are receiving information on discrete issues which can relate to concerns of sexuality and sexual well being. The students recognised that many teachers are uncomfortable teaching sex education and this, they argue, leads to poor quality teaching; the teacher frequently resorting to audio visual aids in order to overcome the necessity of having to teach the subject. In contrast the students acknowledged and appreciated the 'up front' approach of Mrs Pigeon, widely respected by all the students for her open, matter of fact approach.

The students all acknowledged the biological emphasis which is placed on what is taught as sex education. The focus groups made several references to learning about plants (and turtles!). This implies that the students recognise that the emotional and physical aspects of sex education are being ignored in favour of lessons which serve to cover merely the mechanics of reproduction. They seemed to think that they are offered little which is useful or relevant to their needs and lifestyles. In consequence, they had sought alternative sources of information and advice. Young people seem reluctant, in the main, to approach their parents for information, partly from embarrassment but also because they sense that their parents are uncomfortable or unwilling to talk to them about sexuality. Instead they turn to their older siblings, their peers and various media sources for information and advice. However these alternative sources are gendered. Boys indicated that they would look to their friends for information, while girls will sometimes confide in friends, but prefer the anonymity which they feel exists in reading teen magazines for advice. Although there are advice columns in these magazines which are include 'boys' problems and questions, it must be acknowledged that the magazines are marketed for a female readership and teenage boys do not have access to an equivalent male orientated resource.

**The focus group considered**

The experience of using the focus group as a qualitative research method can be compared with that of the tightrope walker, when things go well there is a feeling of exhilaration, when they go badly ... its a long drop! The team work approach proved to be, for me, both a useful research aid and a vital source of moral support. Kate (as moderator) and I shared a real sense of achievement when things went smoothly, we had 'done it', the method had worked as well as, possibly better than, the literature had suggested. However we also shared the anguish of experiencing the group dynamic operating as a powerful sanctioning device. We could only exchange anxious looks during the long agonised periods of prompting and waiting and waiting and prompting ... and waiting and nothing. As a method, this is not to be advocated for the faint hearted!

The failure of the focus group as a suitable method to allow (particularly the NVQ girls) to give voice to their feelings may well have been related to the degree of cohesion among the group. As Deutch (1968) and Schaible and Jacobs (1975) have demonstrated, this can be influenced by and can serve to influence, the degree and nature of communication among the members of a focus group. The following extract from an analytic memo of mine, written during the research gives an indication of the sense of frustration which I experienced:

This session was really hard going, our [Kate and my own] lack of experience in the field really showed today, we were both very anxious and concerned by the endless pauses and blank stares. I wish I was more adept at the use of silence!! This was like trying to get 'blood out of a stone'!. I think the problem must lie with the 'known' sexual history of some of the members of the group. Possibly the others didn't want to be seen to be overtly critical of sexual 'promiscuity'. But they were all so 'cagey'.

(Extract from an analytic memo to self ).

One of the major purposes of focus group research is to allow the researcher to experience the participants' frustrations, satisfactions, fears and rewards (Chouinard and Albert 1990). Many researchers who have experience of using focus groups as a research tool will echo the sentiments of Kitzinger (1994 p.159) when she asks - are they 'method or madness?'. For me, this use of focus group interviews has offered both delight and despair. The method has afforded me the opportunity to witness at first hand the emotions, the humour and the honesty which many young people bring into discussions about social and sexual relationships. However these insights, particularly in respect of the young women in the NVQ class, have also served to depress, frustrate and anger me at the apparent inadequacy of the education system, which had failed to empower them with either a sense of self worth or real control over their lives. The degree of fluency which the various groups exhibited when talking about sex education provides an interesting parallel with discussions on social class with focus groups of teenage girls (Fraser 1988). In that study there were also varying degrees of participation in the debate and Fraser suggests that this owed much to the class based, social distribution of knowledge within the groups. In common with Fraser, my research also provides evidence of what, in some instances, appear to be contradictory, ambiguous statements. However it must be acknowledged that the emphasis which has been placed on what was spoken, or left unsaid, within the group discussions has been achieved as a result of my own interpretations and understandings of the situations.

This chapter has set out to illustrate the use of the focus group interview as a method of qualitative research. It suggests that this approach can be used effectively in order to collect data on sensitive topics. It has demonstrated the approach with reference to what teenagers had to say about their sex education and the ways in which they said it. Significantly, the research has indicated the ways in which the dynamics of gender (and academic route) can affect its value as a method. At times this allowed for a conspiracy of silence which proved deafening in its intensity. By way of contrast, when there was full group participation, the method enabled the all too often muted voice of the adolescent to be clearly heard.

**References**

Allen, I. (1987), *Education in sex and personal relationships. Policy studies institute research report 665,* Oxford, Pinter.

Anyon, J. (1983), Intersections of gender and class. In S. Walker and L.Barton (eds), *Gender, class and education,* Lewes, Falmer. pp.143-163.

Bash, L. and Coulby, D. (1991), *Contradictions and conflict. The 1988 education act in action,* Guildford, Biddles.

Bernstein, B. (1977), *Class, codes and control,* Vol 3, London, Routledge and Kegan Paul.

Bolerued, K., Christopherson, S., and Frank, E. (1990), Girls' sexual choices. Looking for what is right, In C. Gilligan, N, Lyons, and T. Hanmer (eds), *Making connections,* London, Harvard Press. pp.163-182.

Burman, E. (1990), (ed.) *Feminism in psychological practices,* London, Sage.

Canaan, J. (1986), Why a slut is a slut. In H. Varennes (ed.), *Symbolizing America,* Nebraska, University of Nebraska Press. pp.162-183.

Chitty, C. (1994), Sex, lies and indoctrination, *Forum,* 36(1), pp.15-17.

Chouinard, A. and Albert, J. (eds) (1990), *Research perspectives in a world facing AIDS,* Ottawa, International Development Research Centre, pp.50-65.

Coleman, J. (1990), *The nature of adolescence,* (Fourth Edition), London, Routledge.

Delamont, S. (1990), *Sex roles and the school,* (Second Edition), London, Routledge.

Denscombe, M. (1995), Explorations in group interviews, *British Educational Research Journal,* 21(2), pp.131-146.

Department of Health. (1992), *Health of the nation. White Paper,* London, HMSO.

Deutsch. M. (1968), Field theory in social psychology in G. Lindzey and E. Aronson, (eds), *The handbook of social psychology,* (2nd edition), Reading, Addison-Wesley. pp.412-487.

Farrell, C. (1978), *My mother said.* London, Routledge and Kegan Paul.

Fielding, N. (1993), Ethnography in N. Gilbert (ed.) *Researching social life,* London, Sage, pp.155-171.

Fine, M. (1988), Sexuality, schooling and adolescent females: the missing discourse, *Harvard Educational Review,* 5(1), pp.29-53.

Ford, N. (1991), *The socio-sexual lifestyles of young people in the south west of England,* Exeter, Exeter University Press.

Fraser, E. (1988), Teenage girls talking about class, *Sociology* 22 (3), pp.343-358.

Hammersley, M. and Atkinson, P. (1995), *Ethnography: principles in practice,* (2nd edition), London, Routledge.

Her Majesties Inspectorate (HMI) (1986), *Taking stock of secondary schools,* London, Department of Education and Science.

HMSO (1989), *The Children Act 1989,* London, HMSO.

Holland, D.C. and Eisenhart, M.A. (1990), *Educated in romance,* London, University of Chichago Press.

Kitzinger, J. (1994), Focus groups: method or madness? In M. Boulton (ed.), *Challenge and innovation: methodological advances in social research in HIV/AIDS,* London, Francis and Taylor. pp.48-59.

Kreuger, R. (1988), *Focus groups,* London, Sage.

Lees, S. (1986), *Losing out,* London, Heinnemann.

Mac an Ghaill, M (1991), Schooling, sexuality and male power: towards an emancipatory curriculum', *Gender and Education,* 3(3), pp.291-309.

McRobbie, A. (1978), Working class girls and the culture of femininity, *Contemporary cultural studies: women take issue,* London, Hutchinson.

Measor, L. (1989), Are you coming to see some dirty films tonight?', In L. Holly (ed.), *Girls and sexuality,* Milton Keynes, Open University Press. pp.52-71.

Mellanby, A.R.; Phelps, F.A.; Cricton, N.J. and Tripp, J.H. (1995), School sex education: an experimental programme with educational and medical benefits, *BMJ* 311, 12th August 1995, pp.414-41.

Morgan, D. (1988), *Focus groups,* London, Sage.

Pugsley, L.A. (1994), *Sex education and the PSE curriculum,* Unpublished Undergraduate Dissertation, University of Wales Cardiff.

Pugsley, L.A. (1995), *Sex education: ideology and indifference,* Unpublished Masters Thesis, University of Wales Cardiff.

Schaible, T. D. & Jacobs, A. (1975), Feedback 111. Sequence effects, enhancement of feedback acceptance and group acceptance, *Small group behaviour,* 6. pp.151-173.

Scott, L. with Hood, J. Jenks, J. (1994), *Sexwise 11. Sex education in schools,* London, Borough of Hammersmith and Fulham.

Sharpe, S. (1994), *Just like a girl,* London, Penguin.

Stewart, D. W. and Shamdasani, P. N. (1990), *Focus groups theory and practice,* London, Sage.

Strombler, M. (1994), Buddies or slutties: the collective sexual reputation of fraternity little sisters, *Gender and Society,* 8(3), pp.297-323.

Thomson, R. (1994), Moral rhetoric and public health pragmatism: the recent politics of sex education, *Feminist Review* 48, pp.40-60.

Tolman, D.L. (1994), Doing desire. Adolescent girls struggle for/with sexuality. *Gender and Society,* 8(3), pp.324-342.

Trudell, B.N. (1993), *Doing sex education,* London, Routledge.

Willis, P. (1978), *Learning to labour,* Guildford, Biddles.

Winn, S., Roker, D. and Coleman, J. (1995), Knowledge about puberty and sexual development in 11-16 year olds: implications for health and sex education in schools, *Educational Studies,* 3 (1), pp.89-103.

Wolpe, A. M. (1988), *Within school walls: the role of discipline, sexuality and the curriculum,* London, Routledge.

# 8 Men and feminist research

*Mark Jones*

## Introduction

> I don't know why all these bloody researchers have to find
> out what we can and can't do anyway! We know what
> courses we need to go on don't we! - not them for Christ's
> sake! I'm sick to death of being bloody researched!

Liz made this dramatic point half way through a focus group I was holding
with herself and colleagues as part of my research on the pressures practice
nurses face in identifying and meeting their learning needs. On hearing
Liz's outburst I was scared to death - I had been rumbled, my cover had
been blown and my cloak of empathetic research mindedness had been torn
from me. However, looking around the group, and at Liz herself, I
gradually realised that this was not the case. I was not being included in the
castigation of the 'bloody researchers'. But why not? As this chapter
explains, I believe this was due to my adherence to and utilisation of
feminist research principles in investigating this group, and the several
others I worked with. This chapter gives an account of why I feel that it was
legitimate for me (particularly as a man) to utilise a feminist approach in
my work, with an aim of encouraging other researchers to consider and
integrate similar thoughts into their work, or seek to prove why I was
wrong in working with such an assumption.

Working toward a higher degree in health policy (Jones 1993), I had
chosen to study practice nurses' perceptions of their own learning needs,
and how these perceptions were translated into demand for, and provision
of, ongoing education. The subject choice was based upon an hypothesis,
gained from literature review and personal experience of working as an
adviser to practice nurses, that they are concerned about status, their own
expression of competence, and have a whole range of pressures exerted
upon them by their general practitioner (largely male) employers. Practice

nurses have identified that they require skills updating in order to undertake a wider range of activities in the general practice of today (Damant 1991, Mackay 1993), yet they often find it difficult to convince their GP employers of this need. This difficulty translates into GPs refusing to agree that their nurses require any further education (Slaughter 1991); being reluctant to finance practice nurse education (Slaughter 1991, Stilwell 1991, Dewdney 1992, Hancock 1992, Evans, 1993, and Mackay 1993); and refusing to allow practice nurses time to attend educational events, as this reduces their income generation capacity (Saunders 1991, Slaughter 1991, Zuckermann 1992). With practice nurses being, on the one hand, reminded of their professional responsibility to refuse to undertake activities for which they have not received adequate education (UKCC 1992, Pyne 1993), and, on the other, being threatened in some cases with dismissal if they continue to exhort the need for such education (Zuckermann 1992), my hypothesis was that nurses would find it extremely hard to admit to learning needs, particularly through quantitative research methods, such as questionnaire analysis, and that some alternative approach was required to identify and meet their needs.

In a range of studies, practice nurses have been asked to underscore their ability to perform well, describe their educational background, and identify learning needs, yet results suggest that those who have been studied feel dissatisfied with the experience. Nurses have complained of being overburdened by questionnaires, of being frustrated that they could not express their feelings through such a closed format, of rarely getting feedback on the results, and being concerned as to the purpose behind the surveys (for example; Damant 1990, Crawford 1991, Mungall 1992, Atken *et al* 1993, Mackay 1993, Davies 1994). In short, Reinharz's description of the research process (1979 p.95) as almost an analogy of rape did not seem to be that far off the experiences of many practice nurses:

> ...researchers take, hit, and run...intrude into the subjects privacy, disrupt their perceptions, utilise false pretences, manipulate the relationship, and give nothing in return.

Given that I was to consider the pressures placed upon practice nurses to perform tasks for which they may not have been adequately prepared, and their obvious reluctance to admit this, a methodological approach was needed which did not place the nurses I was to work with in a position of power imbalance or fear of disclosure. They were not to take part in a research process over which they had no control, which offered them no feedback nor assistance, and which sought only to address the agenda set by the researcher for the purpose of attaining his degree, rather than offering an explanation and perhaps some solutions to the real problems they face. As with my readings of Rheinharz, given the position of practice nurses vis-à-vis their profession's view of their deviance, and their GP employers ability to sanction access to education, Mies' opinion also seemed to have resonance:

> Research, which so far has been an instrument of dominance and legitimation of power elites, must be brought to serve the interests of dominated, exploited and oppressed groups, particularly women.
>
> (1983 p.123)

As I pursued the selection of an appropriate methodology from which to give practice nurses equality and voice in the research process, I came to see the adoption of feminist principles as the way forward. Reinharz (1984) indicates that, emerging from the trend in feminist critique of the research process, there came the realisation of a need to study women in terms of their strengths, and not simply as victims (as some supposedly well-intentioned studies had done during this period). This seemed to be a particularly relevant point, given that my hypothesis contained the possibility of victimisation of practice nurses by their GP employers. Concentrating on these women as victims with whom we should sympathise, and so excuse some of their actions revealed during the research (for example giving intentionally misleading questionnaire responses) was to be avoided at all costs. Rather I wanted an approach which would demonstrate their strengths and positive contribution, as Reinharz (1984) intimated, in the face of their potential victimisation.

Given the frustration that practice nurses seemed to have with traditional research processes, and their objectives, it seemed that a methodology had to be found which would let these women really speak. Moreover, in addition to the questions I believed needing answering, I also needed to try and find the questions for which they themselves required answers. Perhaps the questions which have been asked of practice nurses to date, particularly concerning their educational needs, were simply the wrong questions, or at best had been asked in the wrong way. If so, using a feminist research strategy could hopefully lead to a point when participants could formulate and address the questions they want answered, with me as a researcher facilitating this, rather than asking a whole series of questions which may be equally irrelevant to their experience. I believed that a feminist approach was the right one, so what did it really involve?

## Feminist research

Whilst recognising that 'feminism' takes many forms, Smith (1988, p.28) views the feminist critique as,

> social investigations which do not render women and girls invisible but which seek to highlight social issues from the standpoint of women

Stanley (1990 p.12) describes 'feminist methodology' as a broad sense term, concerning itself with the way in which the researcher positions her/himself, the topic she/he sets out to investigate, the method/s or technique/s used, the purposes of the research, and the form and style it is written in. Essentially then, a feminist methodology is about levelling the potential power imbalance between researched and researcher. It is about admitting that the researcher has her (or his) own agenda, and that is intertwined with the lives and experiences of those being researched. It is about allowing participants in the research process to participate fully - to speak in their own voice, to be heard and listened to by someone who understands and who can fully represent that voice. Feminist methodology then, is the underpinning structural theory delineanating a research approach intended to give equality to the participants, and allowing them to use the research process to address the question as they see it, rather than simply providing the answers the researcher may require. The methods chosen; my case, focus group research, were to be used in a way which embodies this principle.

To understand how this operates in practice, we can look at what a feminist methodology is not. The approach is not "orthodox" in terms of traditionally accepted research parlance, in that it challenges conventional approaches to addressing the research question, such as preserving the distance between the researcher and the passive subject, and the patriarchal bias evident in the construction of most methodological theory. These two challenges are particularly relevant, in that the participant group for this research project were all women, drawn from a section of the nursing profession - practice nursing - which is an almost exclusive female occupation. A national census of practice nurses (Atkin and others, 1993 p.18) determined that 99.99% of practice nurses were female, whilst other sources (e.g. Royal College of Nursing, 1990) would indicate that only around half a dozen men are employed as practice nurses within the UK. These women are generally employed by male general practitioners, who may have certain ideas concerning their power and control over their nurse employees. The relationship between GPs and their nurse employees reflects the social divisions approach to the subordination of nurses, specifically the familial model with doctor seeing himself as dominant father, and nurse in the subordinate role of caring mother (see Carpenter 1993 for an overview).

In the mid-seventies, some of the then newly emerging feminist works examining gender in the workplace (for example Frieze, *et al*, 1978) began to demonstrate that patriarchal bias in nearly every academic discipline had actually reproduced gender based oppression. It is important to note that this critique was part of women's general attack on social conventions, particularly in medical practice, in which aspects such as hiring of staff, theory, methods, and teaching practices - including so-called objective methods - were condemned for their sexist nature (see particularly, Boston Women's Health Book Collective, 1973). Mies sees these challenges to established methodological approaches as being an inevitable consequence of the assertion of women in society and rejection of such tenets:

> Thesis: when women begin to change their situation of exploitation or oppression, then this change will have consequences for the research areas, theories, and concepts of methodology of studies which focus on women's issues
>
> (Mies, 1993 p.67)

Mies (1993) believes that the condescending study of women as a dominated, exploited, and oppressed group, needs to be turned around, with research being used for them, not as an instrument of dominance and legitimation of (essentially male) power elites. She sees this as being a tough battle though, and challenges women scholars who want to do more than just a paternalistic 'something for their poorer sisters' (because they feel as a privileged group they are already liberated, but who struggle against a patriarchal system), to take their struggles to the street and participate in the social struggles of the feminist movement.

The thesis of feminist researchers, defining a new methodology which will give women their voice, flies in the face of much of accepted research practice. In particular, it seeks to negate the concept of an impartial researcher probing around with his subjects. Oakley (1981) quotes Moser as an example of the approach to research held by 'traditionalists':

> ...there is something to be said for the interviewer who, while friendly and interested does not get too emotionally involved with the respondent and his problems.
>
> (Moser, 1958, pp.187-8)

In direct contrast to Moser's advice, Harding (1987) indicates that whilst studying women is not new, studying them from the perspective of their own experiences, so that they can understand themselves and the world, can claim virtually no history at all. Such a situation arises, she believes, only through the best feminist analysis when the inquirer is placed in the same critical plane as the subject matter. Harding's argument is developed to suggest that the class, 'race', culture, and gender assumptions, beliefs and behaviour of the researcher her/himself must be placed within the frame of the picture that she/he attempts to paint (Harding, 1987 p.9). Following this philosophy, the researcher is not Moser's detached non-entity, but a real, historical individual with concrete specific desires and interests. The beliefs and values of the researcher are then part of the empirical evidence for (or against) the claims advanced in the results of the research. Reinharz (1986) also believes that it is essential to consider the persona of the researcher, particularly if ways are to be found to approach women as 'actors-in-the-world' rather than objects of other people's actions. Ways of listening to and hearing female language and recognising the damaging way men speak of women are called for. This is only to be achieved through researchers acknowledging their own beliefs and being receptive to what women are telling them. As Reinharz (1986, p.39) suggests 'It was necessary for researchers to state their premises rather than hide them'.

Roberts (1981, p.41) argues that when a feminist interviews women, the use of prescribed interviewing practice is morally indefensible. The goal of finding out about people through interviewing is best achieved when the relationship of interviewer and interviewee is non-hierarchical, and when the interviewer is prepared to invest his or her own personal identity in the relationship. Roberts feels that by adopting a feminist approach, the interview is changed from being a data collection instrument for researchers, to a data collecting instrument for those whose lives are being researched. Hammersley (1992, p.189) identifies this as a key theme of feminist methodology, underlining Mies' (1986, p.126) prerequisite that researchers purporting to adopt such an approach must work in partnership with the researched and 'give their research tools to the people'.

We should also note, however, that some commentators, such as Hammersley (1992), Clegg (1988), and Stacey (1988), observe that the principles described above are not only to be found in some exactly defined 'feminist methodology'. Hammersley identifies the validity of experience against method, the rejection of hierarchy in the research realtionship, and the emancipation of participants as a goal of the research, as the identifying marks of what is claimed to be a feminist methodology, yet he asserts that other methodologies exhibit these traits also (1992, pp.202-203). Similarly, Clegg (1988, p.94) argues against the formulation of a specific feminist methodology, 'in the sense of a set of defined epistemological and/or methodological reconstructions', seeing such an attempt as 'not only misguided, but in danger of missing what feminists have really contributed'.

In approaching my research, I did not set out to define a discreet feminist methodology. What I did do though, was identify a number of key principles, as described above, which so obviously derived from a feminist philosophy. Whilst acknowledging that one must guard against claiming these principles as only being represented by a strictly defined feminist methodology, it was clear to me that they were the product of the contribution of feminists to developing the research process, and that a feminist methodological approach could indeed be identified. This certainly seemed to be the approach I wanted, and needed, to adopt.

Only one problem remained for me, and it was a pretty big one at that - I am a man. My reading on the use of feminist principles in research greatly appealed to me. Yet I could not help having an overriding doubt that at best I had no legitimacy in this due to the constraints of my sex, gender, and experience. At worst I was concerned that utilising such a strategy - as a man - might serve to undermine my reasons for choosing it, specifically the removal of any perceived or actual power imbalance between male researcher and female particpant, and the ideal of the researcher being able to relate directly to the experience of those being researched. At this point, my neat description of methodological selection came to an abrupt halt. I sought to investigate my growing self-doubt and worried that I could not do my research partners - the practice nurses with whom, I would work - the justice they deserved. I set out therefore to prove to myself that this should not be the case.

### Can men be feminist researchers?

Harding (1987) promotes the principle that it is the nature of the research and the way it is done which sets it apart as feminist, rather than the sex of the researcher. For example, she cites the work of John Stewart Mill, Karl Marx, and Friedrich Engels, as all having made feminist contributions, *albeit* imperfect, whereas women such as Marable Morgan and Phylis Schafly exhibit strong misogynistic traits. Harding sees this as demonstrating that 'neither the ability or the willingness to contribute to feminist understanding are sex-linked traits' (Harding, 1987, p.11). Furthermore, Harding is quick to point out that it is those who do not recognise women's agenda who do feminism a disservice, rather than this being a strictly male prerogative:

> Whether they are women or men, those who do not actively
> struggle against the exploitation of women in everyday life
> are unlikely to produce social research about anysubject at
> all that is undistorted by sexism and androcentrism.
>
> (Harding, 1987, p.12).

Reinharz (1992) adds to Harding's view that men can be empathetic so far as the feminist research agenda is concerned; in that some men have understood the critique that feminists developed and are using it to critically evaluate and guide their own work. However Reinharz points out that feminists are divided as to whether any man can call himself a feminist, and as such there is no great call amongst feminists that men should 'do' feminist research. Going further, Reinharz acknowledges that some feminists believe that out of respect for women, men should not write about feminism, and that it is not appropriate for men to write about women.

When it is acknowledged that there may be some merit in men engaging in feminist research, the terms of that acknowledgement may not be necessarily appealing to the male researcher. For example, Harding feels that it is important that men get involved, as it is useful for women to consider research undertaken by the 'oppressor' group (1987 p.10). For his part, Joseph Boone (1992) makes an interesting case that having men, as homosexuals, partake in feminist research actually diminishes the threat felt amongst women that men's desire to be feminist is an heterosexual desire of appropriation.

Faced with these varied, and often polarising views, it was easy to be discouraged at the thought of attempting to use a feminist methodology, for what I believed to be valid reasons, yet face the possible condemnation from the group - women - I was trying to work and engage with as part of the 'conscientization' process which Mies describes (1993, p.72). Doubts grew stronger in the light of Reinharz's (1992, p.429) claim that many male scholars take what she sees as a 'liberal approach' that someone should 'do feminist research', but they feel they have neither personal responsibility for it, nor wish to be directly associated with it. Meyers (1988, p.20) substantiates this view, with her claim that 'many male scholars support and even applaud research with a feminist perspective; relatively few engage in such research'.

If the concerns about being criticised for taking on board a feminist approach were not enough, the thought of adverse judgement from academia *per se* added to it. Meyers (1988) reports that there are still many feminist academics (women) who are afraid to discuss feminism or do feminist research, lest they suffer punishment. This punishment was seen to vary from the inability to get a paper published, to the withdrawal or denial of research funding. My concern here was of the risk of being condemned twice over: not only for purloining a methodology which did not belong to me, but, if women feminists had suffered for undertaking unorthodox research, would I also be frowned upon for selecting such a deviant approach myself?

In addition to the issue of whether men can actually be feminist researchers, is the question of whether they can be any good at it. Lorber and Millman (cited in Millman and Kanter 1987, p.35), point to the difficulties of male sociologists doing research with women. As they see it, men have a serious handicap in that they are frequently unable to 'take the role of' their female subjects. Male actors and subjects are portrayed by male sociologists with loving empiricism, so that we 'see the world through their eyes, watch them in the process of defining, coping, interacting'. However, researchers have often been unable to achieve the same empathy with female subjects. This ability (or inability) of a male researcher to empathise with women participants is a key point. Finch shows in her study (1993), that women were pleased to be a part of research undertaken by a woman. However Finch queries the extent to which the ease of interviewing women is down to the researcher being a women, or simply the interview style. She does suggest that, when a woman is interviewing women the situation has special characteristics which are conducive to the easy flow of information (Finch 1993, p.168). Finch believes this argument is justified in three ways. Firstly through her belief that women are more used to having questions asked of them about private parts of their lives, by the doctor, health visitor, midwife, than men. Secondly, that as subjects of research, women are more likely than men to find questions which express an interest in their lives as unusual, and as such are more likely to accept a woman researcher as a friendly guest rather than inquisitor. The model is in effect one of an easy, intimate relationship between women. Finally, due to the structural position of women in society, particularly their consignment to the privatised domestic sphere, Finch sees them as more likely to welcome the opportunity to talk to a listener who is perceived to be sympathetic. On further analysis though, Finch admits that there are too few accounts of the research/interview process which consider the relationship of gender of interviewer to respondent to enable firm conclusions to be drawn. She does indicate, though, that woman-woman interviewing is political as well as methodological. That is, however effective a male interviewer may be at getting women interviewees to talk, there is still an additional dimension when the interviewer is a woman, because both parties share a subordinate structural position by virtue of their gender. Gender politics aside, she translates this into the stark reality that:

> From an entirely instrumental point of view as a researcher, there are of course great advantages to be gained from capitalizing upon one's shared experiences as a woman.
>
> (Finch 1993, p.172)

In considering this whole issue of what can be described as feminist standpoint epistemology (Harding 1987, Stanley and Wise 1990), Hammersley relates the assertion that only women have the insight to research with women to arguments ascribing privileged insight to other groups (1992 p.193). For example, claims that only a black person can understand other black people (Merton 1972), and the belief advanced by Nazi scientists that only those of Aryan ancestry have access to authentic scientific knowledge, and that the theory of relativity should therefore be dismissed as 'Jewish Science' (Merton 1972, p.12), are all advanced by Hammersley as examples of how we cannot infer any superiority on the part of the researcher based upon a genetic criterion. Rather, the emphasis should be placed on the ability of the researcher to engage in the research process with a knowledge and understanding of oppressed groups, the motives of oppressors, and the reality of experience of those in oppressed groups.

Having considered these various points of view I had to decide whether or not I could legitimately approach my work from a feminist perspective, and even if I did, whether my motives were sound. In fact I had to engage in a good deal of the soul searching, an indulgence which Harding (1987) warns against. As an heterosexual male, I did not represent the diminished threat as perceived by Joseph Boone (1992), yet in myself I still did not feel too comfortable at being about to produce research as a member of Harding's oppressor group. There is literature relating to another male nurse turned researcher, which indicates that being a man is of secondary importance to being identified as a nurse when undertaking research with female colleagues (Porter 1991). Just as Porter had found in his observational studies of nurses working in a ward environment, I found that my position as a (male) researcher - one which had been overtly described to all those taking part in my focus group exercises - was subsumed by the way in which the practice nurses saw me not as a dispassionate, detached, impersonal presence, but rather someone they trusted, believed in, and felt comfortable talking to. That the members of the focus groups related to me in this way is illustrated in the following data extracts.

1.  Mark, its like this love, if we want to go on courses for things that aren't in the contract, we can't...you know what I'm talking about...

2.  I know you understand what it's like Mark...but it is really difficult to stand up and fight when you have to do the job

3.  MJ:     Can you say a little bit more about what you mean?

  Nurse 1    Come on, you know what we are saying...you know how we feel...

  MJ:     I might have an idea about what you are talking about, but I really want to hear you say these things for yourself...

  Nurse 2    ...for the tape you mean!

  MJ:     Yes, for the tape, but not just that, because, er, it is your feelings I really want to know about - how you see it, you see?

  Nurse 1:    OK, I know what you mean, you've got to see though that it is not everyone we can say

these things to, I mean we are taking risks
here you know...

MJ:        I understand that, what you say here is
confidential...

I do not include these quotations as an act of arrogance or simply just to 'prove the point', but rather to emphasise that the Harding (1987) thesis seemed to hold true. In other words, it is the nature of the research and the way it is done which sets it apart as feminist, rather than the sex of the researcher. The possession of the Y chromosome need not render every man incapable of deviating from the objective/quantative path of masculine science. More than anything though, I believed that I could use this methodology as a result of my personal experience of working in a context in which I had already stepped outside of my own gender stereotype. For the last fifteen years of my life I had been a male nurse. My workplace, and in fact my social situation, was dominated by female values, values which I had embraced and shared. Some feminists may argue that this is not possible and that I will always represent the oppressor. However I believed that I could incorporate feminist principles into my research methodology, not as a tokenistic exercise, nor as an 'interesting' thing to attempt, but rather because they were principles I espoused in my life.

My analysis, then, is that men can utilise feminist methodology, but just as only some men can espouse feminist principles and be genuine, so only some men can be feminist researchers. A title which once drew my attention at a railway station bookstand was the *'Bluffers Guide to Feminism'* (I never read it so don't have the bibliographic details!), and it is true that the vocabulary of feminist methodology and social inquiry is not that difficult to learn. Just as anyone can pick up a paintbrush and claim to be an artist, only through an examination of the results can we agree with that claim. Just so with men and feminist research. The principles can be applied, but only by examining the results of the inquiry can we see whether the researcher really understood his materials, the paint he had chosen, the medium he was working with, and the image he had chosen to represent. Is the product a vivid, accurate, and telling composition, one which reflects the reality of experience of those who partnered him in the research process (the sample)? My challenge was not to merely render a faithful reproduction of a feminist approach, just as some artists are capable of copying the old masters, which I could then hang in my gallery as a 'ticked off' achievement (my Masters degree pass). Rather, my challenge was to paint the genuine article, one which reflected a growth of understanding in myself and the nurses who had worked with me.

## Conclusion

It is perhaps reasonable to say that the efficacy of my research, and the use of a feminist approach (particularly as a man) should be judged by feedback from those who actually participated - the nurse members of the focus groups. On completion of the work, an abstract and letter of thanks was sent to all participants. In doing so I was mindful of the comments of a practice nurse adviser friend of mine, who, on reading my research proposal, my friend had commented '...so you will be able to say that you found us all out then'. This comment arose from the aim of ascertaining whether or not practice nurses knowingly gave false answers to questionnaires concerning their competence. How would the participants react on reading the abstract?

From 46 participants, I received back eight letters and twelve telephone calls about my research, including six requests for the full text of the study. Typical comments were:

> Thank you ever so much for letting me take part ... it was really good to talk about how we feel ... to someone who is listening ... I enjoyed doing the group ... once we got chatting it was great to deal with the issues ... and know that we weren't going to get grassed up!

> ... the thing is Mark, we all told it like it is ... but what can we do about it? ... I mean we can't tell it like this can we?

All the participants who responded reported a positive, if not cathartic experience. However it was comments such as the last one (above) which best summed up the research for me. The participants had been honest but in doing so had made themselves vulnerable. Stacey's observation (1988, p.23) that 'the lives, loves, and tragedies that fieldwork informants share with a researcher are ultimately data, grist for the ethnographic mill, a mill that has true grinding power' seems highly relevant. My research conclusions had to be used to support the practice nurse struggle and grind down their 'oppressors' - not the participants themselves - should it be adversely reported. In an attempt to pay back the participants I chose to publish a paper based on my work in one of their major journals *Practice Nurse* (Jones, 1995, p.681-684). Again, this resulted in very positive correspondence, and most telling, a letter from the education department of the UKCC (the professional body for nursing) stating how much easier my study had made it to understand the true position of practice nursing. Other papers (including this one) are in progress, and will hopefully have similar consequences. Of course, these results could well have been achieved by other methodological approaches and methods. However, I believe the feminist principles which allowed the nurses to play an active part in the process, and freely discuss their work and concerns, contributed fully to these successful outcomes.

Importantly though, and without wishing to sound 'corny' or indeed patronising, men who embark on a feminist research project should consider this both a privilege and a learning experience. If, as Harding suggests, the efforts of male feminist researchers could be considered to be the fruits of labour of the 'oppressor group' (1987 p.10), it is perhaps surprising that any group of women would allow men to undertake research with them at all, particularly over a subject so loaded with gender imbalance as the position of the practice nurse vis-à-vis patriarchal medical models and mainly male GP employers. This underlines a conclusion that as a man one can never be a true feminist (in that it is impossible to live and breathe the principles one is espousing). It is essential honestly to acknowledge this in seeking to gain legitimacy and acceptance that it is reasonable for a man to utilise feminist research strategies.

One must also be grateful for the learning experience. As I embarked upon my study, I soon realised that undertaking this piece of work was not just going to be a means to an end - of achieving a degree and answers to my research question - but that I would also learn a good deal from the process. Boone (1992, p.29) observed that:

> Men with a commitment to feminist politics need to be willing to forge self-definitions of themselves as men that make room for the acknowledgement of a difference and a sexuality that is truly heterogeneous.

I was willing to forge, and in doing so learnt much about myself. Principles I had previously accepted, and many of which I had no prior notion of were incorporated into my consciousness. Much of the dissonance I felt as a straight man in a female world was alleviated. Through dealing with the issue of whether or not I could or should use a feminist approach to my work, I realised that I neither should nor could pretend to be a woman so far as my value systems and outlook on life are concerned. Rather I realised that it was possible to be a feminine man, allowing that side of myself which had been suppressed by years of socialisation to become a normal part of me. Ultimately though, even after reassuring myself along these lines, and checking out my assumptions with women friends and colleagues, I was mindful that I would never be gender neutral. Morgan (1981, p.95) seemed to 'hit the nail on the head', with his assertion that:

> Men have to work against the grain - their grain, in order to free their work from sexism, to take gender into account. The male researcher needs, as it were, a small voice at his shoulder reminding him at each point that he is a man.

So, for any would be male-feminist researchers out there - listen for your small voice, and take heed when it comes.

### References

Atkin K., Lunt N., Parker G., and Hirst M.  (1993), *Nurses count: a national census of practice nurses.* York, Social Policy Research Unit, University of York.

Boone. J.A. (1992), Of me(n) and feminism: who(se) is the sex that writes? in Porter D. (ed.) *Between men and feminism.* London, Routledge.pp. 162-193.

Boston Women's Health Book Collective. (1973), *Our bodies, ourselves.* New York, Simon and Schuster.

Carpenter M. (1993), The subordination of nurses in health care: towards a social divisions approach. in Riska E. and Wegar K. (eds) *Gender and work in medicine.* London, Sage ,pp.95-130.

Clegg S. (1988), Feminist methodology - fact or fiction? *Quality and Quantity,* 19(1) pp.83-97.

Damant M. (1990), *Report of the review group for education and training for practice nursing: the challenges of primary health care in the 1990's.* London, English National Board for Nursing, Midwifery, and Health Visiting.

Davies G. (1994), Meeting needs. *Practice Nursing.* 22 March - 04 April p.19.

Dewdney E. (1992), The search for consensus. *Practice Nurse.* June. pp.79-80.

Evans J. (1992), PNs - a picture. *Practice Nursing.* September. p.9.

Finch J. (1993), It's great to have someone to talk to: ethics and problems in interviewing women. In Hammersley M. *Social research, philosophy, politics and practice.* London, Sage, pp.166-180.

Freize I., Talcott Parsons J., Johnson P., Rubie D.,and Zellman G. (1978), *Women and sex roles: a social psychological perspective.* New York, W.W. Norton.

Hancock. C. (1992), Quality in education, *Practice Nursing,* May, p.41.

Hammersley M. (1992), On feminist methodology, *Sociology,* 26, May pp187-206.

Harding S.(ed.) (1987), *Feminism and methodology.* Bloomington, Indiana, Indiana University Press and Milton Keynes, Open University Press.

Jones M. (1993), *I'm not sure I can answer that...an investigation into the suitability of questionnaire survey as a method for ascertaining the learning needs of practice nurses.* Unpublished Masters Degree Dissertation. University of Bristol.

Jones M. (1995), Trip the training trap, *Practice Nurse,* 03 February. pp. 681- 684

Mackay J. (1993), A tender subject, *Practice Nursing,* 21 September - 04 October. pp.18-19.

Merton R.K. (1972), Insiders and outsiders, *American Journal of Sociology,* 78. pp9-47.

Meyers C. (1988), *Discovering Eve: ancient Israelite women in context,* New York, Oxford University Press.

Mies M. (1993), Towards a methodology for feminist research in Hammersley M. (ed.) *Social research, philosophy, politics, and practice,* London, Sage, pp.64-82.

Millman M. and Kanter R.M. (1987), Another voice: feminist perspectives on social life and social science, in Harding. S. (ed.) *Feminism and methodology,* Bloomington, Indiana, Indiana University Press & Milton Keynes, Open University Press, pp.29-36.

Morgan D. (1981), Men, masculinity, and the process of sociological enquiry, in Roberts H. (ed.) *Doing feminist research,* London, Routledge.pp.83-113.

Moser C.A. (1958), *Survey methods in social investigation,* London, Heinemann.

Mungall I. (1992), The road to better training, *Practice Nurse,* May, pp.56-61.

Oakley A. (1981), Interviewing women, a contradiction in terms, in Roberts. H. (ed.) *Doing feminist research,* London, Routledge and Kegan Paul. pp.30-61.

Porter S. (1991), A participant observation study of power relations between nurses and doctors in a general hospital, *Journal of Advanced Nursing,* 16, pp.728-735.

Pyne R. (1993), Frameworks, *Practice Nursing,* 21 September - 04 October, pp.14-15.

Reinharz S. (1979), *On becoming a social scientist: from survey research and participant observation to experiential analysis,* San Francisco, Jossey-Bass.

Reinharz S. (1984), Women as competent community builders: the other side of the coin, in Gerrard M., Iscue I., and Rickel A. (eds) *Social and psychological problems of women,* New York, Macmillan, pp.19-43.

Reinharz S. (1986), Patriarchal pontifications, *Transaction/Society,* 23 (6) pp.23-39.

Reinharz S. (1992), The principles of feminist research - a matter of debate, in Kramarae C., and Spender D. (eds) *The knowledge explosion: generations of female scholarship,* New York, Teachers College Press, pp.423-447.

Roberts H. (ed.) (1981), *Doing feminist research,* London, Routledge and Keegan Paul.

Royal College of Nursing of the United Kingdom. (1990), *Characteristics of nurses employed in general practice,* Unpublished Survey, RCN Community Health Nursing.

Saunders M. (1991), Stand up for yourselves! *Practice Nursing,* January, p.20.

Slaughter S. (1991), Practice nursing profile: Susan Slaughter, *Practice Nursing,* November. p.2.

Smith D. (1988), *The everyday world as problematic,* Milton Keynes, Open University Press.

Stacey J. (1988), Can there be a feminist ethnography? *Women's Studies International Forum,* 11(1) , pp. 21-27.

Stanley L. (ed.) (1990), *Feminist praxis,* London, Routledge.

Stanley L. and Wise S. (1990), Method, methodology, and epistemology in feminist research processes, in Stanley L. (ed.) *Feminist Praxis,* London, Routledge,pp.20-62.

Stilwell B. (1991), Practice nurses role needs further definition, *Practice Nurse,* January, p.466.

United Kingdom Central Council for Nursing, Midwifery and Health Visiting. (1992), *Code of professional conduct, for nurses, midwives, and health visitors,* London, United Kingdom Central Council for Nursing, Midwifery and Health Visiting.

Zuckerman C. (1992), Jobs may be under threat, *Practice Nursing,* September. p.1.

# 9 Time for feminist approaches to technology, 'nature' and work

*Barbara Adam*

## Introduction

For feminist social scientists time has become a pertinent political issue. As a conceptual tool, the focus on time not only helps us to establish connections between technology, work and the environment, but also to understand the role of women in those spheres, their invisibility and lack of power as well as their strengths and potential. A focus on time also helps to displace those conceptual tools of the Enlightenment such as the valorization of objectivity and the thinking in terms of binary opposites. It is through a focus on time that we are able to address feminist concerns about essentialism and determinism (Forman, 1989, Forman and Sowton, 1989).

In this article I want to offer a feminist analysis of some of the issues that relate to technology, 'nature' and work using time as a focal point for discussion (Adam,1993, 1995). I am particularly interested in the machine time of clocks and its pervasiveness in social practices, structures and theories. While the traditional response to this pervasiveness has been to contrast machine time with the times of nature, social with body time and men's with women's time, I want to examine instead the multiplicity of times: embedded, embodied, objectified, evaluated and commodified. My analysis considers the implications for feminist praxis of taking an explicit account of time in research on technology, work and the environment.

## Feminism confronts technology

In her excellent study *Feminism Confronts Technology*, Wajcman (1991) shows feminist analyses of technology to present a contradictory and paradoxical picture. While there is agreement on the gendered nature of technology and on an associated inequality of power, there is little consensus on how to understand or respond to those findings. Is the consistent male bias to be sought in differences associated with the respective reproductive capacities of women and men: that is, while women give birth to the next generation of human beings, men give birth to bombs and computers, the next generation of technologies? (Easlea, 1983; Plant, 1989). Is it to be understood in relation to cognitive difference as Turkle (1984) suggests? Or is it to be located in socio-historical and economic constructions and practices, the position with which Wajcman (1991) herself is most comfortable? Are we, she asks, to celebrate our proposed closer identity with nature? Should we seek to infuse technology with our values? Are we to appropriate technology for our own ends, or ensure that we compete on equal terms for the chance to excel not merely in the use of technology, but in its design and construction?

All but the most recent feminist approaches to technology are couched in terms of either-or choices: that is, women as nature and 'other', *or* as capable of technological prowess after the historically sedimented inequalities are removed; essential *or* fractured identities; technology impinging from the outside *or* embedded in social practices at a fundamental level. Despite the fact that feminist writings on technology arose from the critique of an Enlightenment tradition of rational science that constructs reality not only in dualistic but also in hierarchical terms, the responses themselves tend to get reabsorbed into the very frames of meaning they seek to transcend. The dualisms of this classical science still infuse the analyses. 'Culture vs. nature, mind vs. body, reasons vs. emotions, objectivity vs. subjectivity, the public realm vs. the private realm', as Wajcman (1991 p.5) points out, are still the backcloth against which the understandings are constructed. To focus on gendered differences without simultaneously identifying the complexity of similarities across genders is to partake in what Ermarth sees as the perpetual re-inscription of women as 'other', (Ermarth, 1989). Moreover, the metaphor of technology as a 'double-edged sword' (Wajcman, 1991 p.61), and concerns about technological determinism and natural essentialism, hinder the task of overcoming the dualisms through which women are constructed as 'other' to the 'technologically gifted' male. The dual focus on time and technology provides new access points to this debate. I want to look therefore at the time/technology connection - by focusing on its most famous conjuncture: clock time - and to explore the significance of this powerful convergence for the complex and interconnected gendered characteristics of work relations, approaches to the body and, by implication, attitudes to the environment.

**The rise of machine time**

> The clock is both the outstanding fact and the typical symbol
> of the machine: even today no other machine is so
> ubiquitous.
>
> (Mumford, 1955, p.5)

With the aid of the clock, the variable times of nature - of day and night, seasons and change, growth and ageing, birth and death - became objectified, constituted independently of nature and cosmic processes. As a machine whose product - hours, minutes and seconds - is by necessity disconnected from human activity and social organization, the clock facilitated belief in an external reality amenable to measurement and control.

> When one thinks of the day as an abstract span of time, one
> does not go to bed with the chickens on a winter's night: one
> invents wicks, chimneys, lamps, gaslights, electric lamps, so
> as to use all the hours belonging to the day. When one
> thinks of time, not as a sequence of experiences, but as a
> collection of hours, minutes and seconds, the habits of
> adding time and saving time come into existence.
>
> (Mumford, 1955, p.8)

A time that comes in standardized, invariable, infinitely divisible units can be given a number value. As such it can serve as a medium for exchange, as a base to translate one quantity into another. Historical periods can be related to each other, labour can be translated into money and risks can be calculated for insurance purposes. Created externally, clock time can function as a symbol for orientation, regulation and control and it allows us to integrate all levels of reality - cosmic, physical, biological, and cultural - as well as all known historical periods, (Elias, 1992).

Decontextualized, disembodied, specialized (and thus detemporalized), clock time is both a precondition and a vital tool for Newtonian science. As such, it underpins much of what feminist social theorists make problematic: objectivity, abstraction, verification across time and space, standardization, and unifying theories (Duelli Klein, 1983; Ermarth, 1992; Harding, 1986; Harding, 1987; Hekman, 1990; Mies, 1983). For this reason alone, clock time is worth more detailed attention. Focus on the characteristics of this technological time is particularly pertinent, however, because it has become such a taken-for-granted aspect in the daily lives of Western women as well as in the theories we develop about the gendered experiences of those lives:

> It is there, like Mont Blanc; it is given; it is "natural". But such faith is a trick of perspective. Linear time is an artifice. It is, for better or worse, one of the massive achievements of Western culture, and as such is a profoundly collective construct.
>
> (Ermarth, 1992, p.42)

As a 'profoundly collective construct' this time is created, recreated and maintained, to varying degrees and in different ways, by all whose lives are touched by its influence. Is it thus important to break through the 'natural' attitude for a number of reasons: to recognize the metaphorical power of clock time; to appreciate the conflictual relation of clock time to temporalities that are not easily translated into its quantifiable units; to understand the inequalities of power associated with different times; and to realize our potential for change and reconstruction.

The created, technological time of the clock ticks away evenly and objectively. It is linked to abstract motion and to distance travelled in space. It marks time by dissociation, by abstracting it from human events and assigning it a number value. Emphasis on the clock-work highlights mechanical relationships; cogs and springs interacting to form an integrated whole. It accentuates parts. The smooth running of the whole depends on invariable timing, tempo, sequence, duration, and periodicity. As such, the clock is a metaphor for an inanimate reality, for a world locked in predetermined pathways where nothing new ever happens and where cause and effect stand in a proportional relation to each other. It expresses a world of mechanically interacting parts: simple, demystified, measurable and predictable. It represents a reality that can be taken apart and reassembled physically and conceptually. It stands for a controllable reality that constitutes humans in the role of machine operators and makers (see Adam, 1990, chapter 2). Moreover, it is a powerful externalizer that separates subject from object, and individuals from their experiences. As such it facilitates the transformation of contextual, active agents into disembodied, passive observers. Disembedded from the temporalities and chronologies of being, and separated from the past, present and future, time can be used as a social tool for orientation, synchronization and regulation. The multiplicity of temporalities so abstracted is then translatable into a resource, a material commodity to be allocated and controlled. As a conceptual tool and metaphor, furthermore, the clock encompasses a number of principles that underpin scientific theories and designs: the emphasis on abstraction, separation and otherness; the elimination of context; and the allied pursuit of permanence and timeless Truth. It entails the very characteristics that are consistently questioned by feminist social theorists with reference to methodology and epistemology, features that are identified with male tendencies and the imposition of power.

**Embedded times: finite and generated**

To deepen our appreciation of the link between technology and control it will be useful to look beyond clock time to consider how time is embedded in technological artefacts more generally. The products of technology are designed and created apart, frozen for contemplation, fixed in their uniqueness. This applies to cultural products from cave paintings to machines. Their immutability allows us to get to know them. Thus, externalization of knowledge in fixed form allows for contemplation and control in a way that would be quite impossible to achieve for embodied knowledge lived in daily practice. In its objectified, artefactual form, therefore, knowledge is associated with power over nature and fellow human beings. What tends to be identified by eco-feminists as a male way of relating to nature (Griffin, 1981; Merchent, 1980) has to be recognized as intimately tied to the externalization of knowledge in temporally fixed and finite form. This time of cultural products is isolated from the give-and-take of ecological exchange and from the interdependent, variable and transient processes of life and reproduction. It is a time from which body and soul are exorcised. It is a temporality governed by entropy rather than by development and growth, a time of finitude, death and pollution, antithetical to generative being. In contrast to living systems, whose success depends on both their mortality and the transience of their internal subsystems, the products of culture in general, and of technology in particular, are not designed for birth, death and regeneration.

A focus on the embedded times of cultural products and living processes leads us to environmental issues and the gendered approaches to finitude, transcendence and the future. Feminists have argued that the creation of artefacts is the male way of overcoming finitude, linking this male transcendence to the control of nature on one hand, and to environmental problems on the other (Griffin, 1981; King, 1989; Merchant, 1980; Plant, 1989). O'Brien (1981, pp.32-3), for example, contrasts the transcendence of finitude by technological and abstract means with the female principle of continuity through birthing, with the creative utilisation of life and death that extends indefinitely into the past and future, while King (1989 p.21) argues that 'patriarchal civilisation is about the denial of men's mortality - of which women and nature are incessant reminders' (see also Brodribb 1992 and Adam 1995 for a more detailed discussion). We need to be careful, however, that the distinction between two *principles* does not slide into an opposition between male and female *practices*, that is to say into a dualism where we conceive of women ensuring continuity through their creative bodies and men through their analytic minds and hands. What can be stated, is that women's capacity for transcending mortality is grounded not only in artefacts but also in the generative temporality of giving birth. This difference in emphasis is, in turn, reflected in theory. Thus, for Irigaray (1983) and O'Brien (1989), Heidegger's 'Being unto death' signifies the masculine approach to time which they reject. For them such an approach offers an inappropriate perspective on human temporality and the human relationship to nature since it excludes birth and the time-generating capacity of procreation. To reintegrate birth as central to human temporality, they argue, is to find a new relationship to continuity and a 'shift from a death-determined future to a birth-determined one' (Forman, 1989, p.7); it is to foreground aspects of life in our relationship to nature.

We are not dealing with a question of choice: nature *or* culture, environment *or* technology, lived *or* constructed time. Those who give and generate time also live *in* time. They are subject to a complexity of times governed by natural and social rhythms, by culturally set rites of passage, by calendars and clocks. Focusing on time, we recognize that we live, breathe and eat in ways that reflect the rhythms of our planet and that we operate on a daily basis in contexts of socially constructed clock time. This mechanical time is both out of step with the variable cycles of nature and intricately tied to them. Difference has thus to be understood as mutually implicating and needs to be theorized with reference to shared dimensions and characteristics. Thus, focus on the time-artefact-technology connection can help us to overcome dualistic and essentialist tendencies in our theories. Let me illustrate the point through the example of birthing:

> The woman in labour, forced by the intensity of the contractions to turn all her attention to them, loses her ordinary, intimate contact with clock time. This endless rhythm, like the succession of waves at the shore, the murmur of our breathing, the drumbeat of the heart, is a living symbol of the timeless, endless world.
>
> (Fox, 1989, p.127)

As this experience becomes embodied in the woman's being, constituting an integral part of her mindful body, her memory and her consciousness, it forms part of her identity. If fuses her physiological, social, conscious and unconscious Self with an event in which the everyday times of clocks, calendars, schedules and deadlines have no place. And yet for women in many industrialized countries, this archetypal time of the birthing process takes place in a context where clock time reigns supreme. In the labour wards of hospitals everything is measured against the calendar and the clock: the timing of labour and the length of each stage, the baby's heartbeat and the progress in cervical dilation, the lengths of the contractions and their spacing. The more intrusive the obstetric assistance, the more the woman is forced to oscillate between the all-encompassing body time of her labour and the rational framework of her clock-time environment. She has to answer questions, report on her sensations and listen to instructions. Her out-of-rational-time state is at odds with the abstract, ordered world of time measurement, yet managed and constructed into a coherent whole. Taking charge over her time, the attendants transform their exclusion from the centre into a situation of clear purpose and control, translating an unmanageable process of archetypal time into one more closely akin to the manageable chronology of industrial production: first this, then that, at the right time, for pre-set periods, and for the appropriate duration. It seems clear that a woman's entry into the time of her labouring body disrupts the attendants' sense of time, their dependence on the predictability and reliability of clock time, raising for them the spectre of uncertainty, separation and death. Consequently, they reconstruct the situation to the templates of their own untheorized assumptions. That is to say, obstetricians project their time into the birthing event and thus reformulate an archetypal time event into a chronology (see Adam, 1995, chapter 2).

This brief sketch of the body time of birthing in the context of Western-style obstetrics demonstrates the need to conceive of such an event in terms other than the traditional separation of nature from culture, natural from social times. Even the idea of oscillating between two times - the archetypal temporality of the birthing process and the rational clock-time of obstetrics - is misleading since those times interpenetrate and mutually inform each other's meanings. For the attendants, for example, the purity of clock time becomes contaminated as they are drawn into, respond to, and draw back from the archetypal time of birthing. For the woman in labour, the two times blend into each other to constitute a cohesive, mostly unproblematic, whole. Explicit focus on the female body time of birthing thus illuminates the complex interpenetration of the temporalities of social organization, technology and the mindful body (Fox, 1989; Pfeufer Kahn, 1989; Pizzini, 1992; Thomas, 1992). The example shows further that we need to recognize that pre-industrial rhythms are not superseded by industrial ones; archetypal times are not replaced by chronology. Rather, the primordial times persist and permeate our present while the imposed artefactual temporalities affect and subtly transform body and environmental time to a point where we can no longer conceptualize them in a meaningful way as distinct. Just as clock time is permeated by planetary rhythms, so too are body times acculturated and socialized into the metronomic beat of the clock.

Yet this is only part of the story. There is a need for us to understand how women's time of reproduction and their emphasis on birth and regeneration are rendered invisible by the dominant times of calendars and clocks; we need to understand how it is that their time-giving becomes subsumed under time consumption and devalued in the context of economic relations of time. We need to appreciate that generative temporality does not exist in isolation but in an unequal interaction with the construction of permanence through artefacts and symbolic systems, products of science, institutions and market structures. That is, we need to explore the contexts and the grounds on which women find their reproductive lives and their histories constituted in the shadows of the world of production.

Generators of time simultaneously partake in, articulate, and help to maintain the dominant time as a collective construct. Inextricably incorporated into a life of commerce, they inevitably collude in the commodified relations of time in which speed and the economic approach to time are valorized. Within that context, generators and givers of time find it difficult to defend an open-ended time of care and a reduction in pace since their activities are evaluated through criteria based on a finite resource. As the shadows of the world of resource consumption, time-generating interactions are judged on the basis of the abstracted, standardized measure of the clock. Nowhere is this inequality between different temporalities more visible than in the world of work in industrialized countries.


**Working times: orthodoxy and paradoxes**

Marx (1973 [1857]; 1976 [1867]) identified clock time with the alienating process of commodification. Every commodity, including labour power, he argued, is 'the objectification of a given amount of labour time' (Marx, 1973

[1857] p.140). For that to be possible, time had first to be objectified, decontextualized and quantified. That is to say, only as clock time could time be used as an abstract medium for exchange. More recently, Thompson (1967), proposed a distinction between traditional and industrial societies: whereas the time allocations of the former were predetermined by tasks, the time allocations of industrial societies are structured around the clock. In other words, where work used to be the measure of time, today time is the measure of work. Both these approaches were gender blind as was, until recently, most of the literature on time and work. Since the late 1980s, however, feminist researchers on time and work have begun to speak to those silences and have introduced levels of complexity previously unknown in this area of research and theory (Adam, 1993; Adam, 1995; Davies, 1990; Hantrais, 1993; Inhetveen, 1994; Leccardi & Rampazi, 1993; Le Feuvre, 1994; Nowotny, 1990; Pasero, 1994). After first demanding equal rights in and to the linear time of history, and after consequently establishing the fundamental difference between patriarchal and matriarchal time, contemporary feminists are striving to come to terms with the complexities and contradictions posed for women by the dominance of clock time and the emphases on linearity and finitude (Kristeva, 1981). In their quest to transcend the old dualisms, they seek to conceptualize the paradoxes of belonging to a world dominated by the quantitative times of production and death, while orienting towards the generative times of reproduction and life.

Sensitivity to the gendered nature of working time shows that women in industrialized and industrializing countries are both integral to the world of standardized, commodified time and clock-based rhythms, and at odds with those times: they are subject to social time structures, deadlines and schedules. They are tied into an economic life in which labour time is exchanged for money and employment relations are dependent on time as an abstract exchange value. Yet the times of reproduction and nurturing, of caring, loving and educating, of household management and maintenance are not so much time measured, paid, spent, allocated and controlled as time lived, given and generated. Because such time is not easily quantified, it is not suitable for translation into money. This has significant consequences. In a world in which money is synonymous with power, any time that cannon be given a monetary value is by definition associated with a lack of power. We thus need to look more closely at the complex interpenetration of the rationalized, commodified time of the clock and times that operate outside and against the cash nexus.

Davies (1990), in her perceptive and innovative study of Swedish women's experiences, shows how their time cannot be placed in a meaningful way within perspectives that separate work from leisure, public from private activities, and task from clock time. Her work stresses the irreducible complexity of women's times, a complexity that can be reduced neither to simple oppositions, nor to before-and-after statements. Avoiding dualistic conceptions, she is nevertheless able to demonstrate that times which are not convertible into currency have to remain outside the charmed circle: they cannot be evaluated and priced in a system of exchange that equates time with money. As such they are constituted in the shadows of commodified time. In traditional social science analyses they were consequently rendered invisible.

Where research has focused explicitly on women's uses and experiences of time, the data suggest that women as mothers and carers feel themselves on call twenty-four hours a day and that therefore the split of eight hours of work, eight hours of leisure and eight hours of sleep does not apply to the daily structure of their otherwise different lives. The cliche 'women's work is never done' exemplifies the incompatibility of women's time with a work time that can be measured, exchanged for money, accumulated for 'time out', and delimited against leisure time. Irrespective of whether women are in paid employment or whether they have husbands, children and/or elderly parents, the complexity of their times is found to be irreducible to the decontextualized commodity. Often it is mediated and derived time, shared rather than personal time, a relational time that is fundamentally enmeshed with that of significant others. The necessarily open-ended nature of this shared time poses difficulties for the assumption of a uniform, standardized time and for an equality of evaluation within the commodified relations mediated by clock time.

The premise of a smooth, progressive time constitutes a problem not only for the complexity of women's daily time-based activities, but also for assumptions relating to longer-term perspectives on women's working lives. In their study of young Italian women, Leccardi and Rampazi (1993), found characteristics that transcended class and age differences. Their data suggest a plurality of interdependent times, a patchwork that cannot be hierarchically sequenced and ordered. Having to integrate the dual careers of work and homemaker, both with very different ethical orientations, these women experience considerable difficulty in structuring their daily lives as well as substantial 'ambivalence when the time comes for making choices and projecting oneself into the future' (Leccardi & Rampazi, 1993, p.361). This is because choices about careers are not achieved freely and independently, but rather signify an awareness of the intrinsic limit to self direction: '[t]he expectation of biographical events such as falling in love, forming a family, giving birth to and caring for children moulds their representation' (Leccardi & Rampazi, 1993, p.369). A 'known' future to some extent determines the content, the timing and the sequences of the choices: there is, for example, a limited time-span during which women can bear children; there are optimal times at which to start a career. Such temporal judgements are, in turn, tempered by moral and financial considerations. Women talk of juggling their many incompatible times and of creating a 'puzzle of bits and pieces of work and training' (Adam, 1993, p.173). These experiences resonate with feminist writings that challenge the assumption of work as a full-time, continuous occupation with a linear career structure.

An added level of complexity arises once we acknowledge that while time is not gender neutral, both the juggling of a plurality of times, and the time generating and giving associated with caring are not the sole prerogative of women: men too have to integrate what are often incompatible temporal considerations. Some of their time is open-ended and contextual, which means it too falls outside the grasp of quantification, commodification and control. It too is problematic for traditional, clock-time based social science analyses. This becomes most evident when men are engaged in caring activities outside the world of paid employment. Often, men and women of similar structural positions share aspects of their lives that differentiate their temporal experiences from those in paid employment. This discrepancy applies equally to periods of childhood, education, unemployment and retirement, to all the times outside the direct control of the labour market. Shared temporalities and differences thus stand in a complex relation to each other: never simple, never single, never dualistic. In writing about these paradoxes, feminists are giving shape to the invisible. Their attention to those aspects of Western, commercialized social time may help to recover an essential balance between the consumption and the regeneration of time, a time out of sync with 'nature' and temporalities embedded in the creative give-and-take of ecological relations. It is not surprising therefore, that 'to be female', as Forman (1989, p.1) puts it, 'is to have an uneasy relationship to time'. The solution, however, is not to establish a new dualism of male/female times but to understand the principles that underpin the dominant time and its impact, as well as the characteristics of times that fall outside its remit. It is to demystify and to make the taken-for-granted problematic. This in turn creates the potential for alternative visions and for effective actions.

**Implications for feminist theory**

When time is used as a conceptual tool for understanding social life, a number of consequences ensue. Because the focus on time forces us to attend to the complexities of any one moment of interactive observation, the dualisms that play such a powerful role in our theories are being displaced. Thus we note how time is neither bought nor given but used; we see how it is commodified, measured, generated and constructed simultaneously; how past, present and future interpenetrate; and how women's productive-reproductive, public-private and industrial-domestic lives all implicate and constitute each other. Secondly, we see power relations in different terms - globally between nations, and locally between groups and classes of people. We recognize clock time, for example, as a globally-imposed, industrial imperialism; we understand the associated devaluation of all times that are not quantifiable and translatable into a money value, as well as the attendant valorization of speed in relation to this colonizing rationalization process. Thirdly, we understand one of the key bases upon which women and 'nature' are constructed as 'other' within the dominant discourse of Newtonian science and Cartesian philosophy. That is to say, we can see how that which is not objectifiable by artefactual or technological means, and that which cannot be mediated by clock time, falls outside the rationalist framework of Enlightenment thought. We see how it is negated, silenced and constructed as 'other'. Finally, we endeavour to understand the effects of abstract, dismembered historical thinking and the relation to clock time as time *per se* and we begin self-consciously to participate in the construction of time. We appreciate that as temporal, embodied, moral beings we need to let go of the spurious comfort of linear progression, certainty and control and embrace the constitutive nature of our knowledge with all its ramifications. We move from the safety of objectivity to the conscious partiality of implicated participant within and of a world of science and facts. 'Once we begin to see our mental manoeuvres as inventions, they become', as Ermarth (1992, p.23) points out, 'not "neutral" and "natural" ways of behaving but instead modes of exercising responsibility and freedom'. While emphasizing complexity, uncertainty and constitutive reflexivity, the focus on time allows us to ground that fundamental multiplicity in embedded, embodied and contextual knowledge and demonstrates the inescapable responsibility of each of us for the construction not only of our present but of the past and, even more importantly, the future.

## References

Adam, B. (1990), *Time and social theory* Cambridge, Polity.

Adam, B. (1993), Within and beyond the time economy of employment relations *Social Science Information* 32 pp163-184.

Adam, B. (1995), *Timewatch: the social analysis of time* Cambridge: Polity.

Brodribb, S. (1992), The birth of time: generation(s) and genealogy in Mary O'Brian and Lucy Irigary *Time & Society,* 1 pp257-270.

Davies, K. (1990), *Women and time: the weaving of the strands of everyday life* Aldershot, Avebury.

Duelli Klein, R. (1983), How to do what we want to do: thoughts about feminist methodology in G. Bowles and R. Duelli Klein (eds) *Theories of women's studies,* London, Routledge & Kegan Paul, pp88-104.

Easlea, B. (1983), *Fathering the unthinkable: masculinity, scientists and the nuclear arms race,* London, Pluto Press.

Elias, N. (1992), *Time an essay,* Oxford, Blackwell.

Ermarth, E.D. (1989), 'The solitude of women and social time' in F.J. Forman and C. Sowton (eds) *Taking our time: feminist perspectives on temporality,* Oxford, Pergamon, pp37-46.

Ermarth, E.D. (1992), *Sequel to history: postmodernism and the crisis of representational time,* Princeton, Princeton University Press.

Forman, F.J. (1989), Feminizing time: an introduction in F.J. Forman and C. Sowtown (eds) *Taking our time: feminist feminism* Philadelphia: New Society Publishers. pp. 1-9.

Forman, F.J. and Sowton, C. (eds) (1989), *Taking our time: feminist perspectives on temporality,* Oxford, Pergamon.

Fox, M. (1989), Unreliable allies: subjective and objective time in F.J. Forman and C. Sowton (eds) *Taking our time: feminist perspectives on temporality,* Oxford, Pergamon, pp123-135.

Griffin, S. (1981), *Women and nature,* New York, Harper and Row.

Hantrais, L. (1993), The gender of time in professional occupations *Time & Society* 2 pp139-157.

Harding, S. (1986), *The science question in feminism,* New York, Cornell University Press.

Harding, S. (1987), Introduction: is there a feminist method? in S. Harding (ed.) *Feminism and Methodology,* Bloomington, Indiana University Press, pp1-14.

Hekman, S.J. (1990), *Gender and knowledge: elements of a postmodern feminism,* Cambridge, Polity.

Inhetveen, H. (1994), The times of farming women *Time & Society*, 3 pp.259-276.

Irigaray, L. (1983), *L'Oubi de l'air, chez Martin Hedegger*, Paris, Les Editions de Minuet.

King, Y. (1989), The ecology of feminism and the feminism of ecology in J. Plant (ed.) *Healing the wounds: the promise of eco-feminism*, Philadelphia, New Society Publishers, pp18-28.

Kristeva, J. (1981), Women's time trans A. Jardine and H. Blake *Signs*, 7 pp5-35.

Leccardi, C. and Rampazi, M. (1993), Past and future in young women's experience of time, *Time & Society*, 2 pp358-380.

LeFeuvre, N. (1994), Leisure, work and gender: a sociological study of women's time in France, *Time & Society*, 3 (2) pp.151-178.

Marx, K. (1973) [1867] *Grundisse*, Harmondsworth, Penguin.

Marx, K. (1976) [1867] *Capital Volume 1*, Harmondsworth, Penguin.

Merchant, C. (1980) *The death of nature: women, ecology and the scientific revolution*, New York, Harper Row.

Mies, M. (1983) Towards a methodology of feminist research in G. Bowles and Duelli Klein (eds) *Theories of women's studies*, London, Routledge & Kegan Paul, pp117-139.

Mumford, L. (1955) *The monastery and the clock: the human prospect*, Boston, Beacon Press, pp3-10.

Nowotny, H. (1990) *The public and private uses of time: in search of usable knowledge*, Frankfurt, Campus Westview, pp29-36.

O'Brien, M. (1981) *The politics of reproduction*, London, Routledge and Kegan Paul.

O'Brien, M. (1989) Resolute anticipation in Heidegger and Beckett (eds) *Reproducing the world: essays in feminist theory*, Boulder, Westview Press, pp83-101.

Pasero, U. (1994) Social time patterns, contingency and gender relations, *Time & Society*, 3 (2), pp.179-192.

Pfeufer Kahn, R. (1989) Women and time in childbirth and during lactation in F.J. Forman and C. Sowton (eds) *Taking our time: feminist perspectives on temporality*, Oxford, Pergamon, pp20-36.

Pizzini, F. (1992) Women's time, institutional time in R. Frankenburg (ed.) *Time, health and medicine*, London, Sage, pp68-74.

Plant, J. (1989) (ed.) *Healing the wounds: the promise of eco-feminism*, Philadelphia, New Society Publishers.

Thomas, H. (1992) Time and the cervix in R. Frankenberg (ed.) *Time, health and medicine*, London, Sage, pp56-67.

Thompson, E.P. (1967) Time, work-discipline and industrial capitalism *Past and Present,* 36 pp52-97.

Turkle, S. (1984) *The second self: computers and the human spirit,* London, Granada.

Wajcman, J. (1991) *Feminism confronts technology,* Cambridge, Polity.